THE
BULLY-FREE
WORKPLACE

THE BULLY-FREE WORKPLACE

STOP JERKS, WEASELS, and SNAKES FROM KILLING YOUR ORGANIZATION

GARY NAMIE
RUTH F. NAMIE

WILEY

John Wiley & Sons, Inc.

Published by John Wiley & Sons, Inc., Hoboken, New Jersey.
Published simultaneously in Canada.

Limit of Liability/Disclaimer of Warranty: While the publisher and author have used their best efforts in preparing this book, they make no representations or warranties with respect to the accuracy or completeness of the contents of this book and specifically disclaim any implied warranties of merchantability or fitness for a particular purpose. No warranty may be created or extended by sales representatives or written sales materials. The advice and strategies contained herein may not be suitable for your situation. You should consult with a professional where appropriate. Neither the publisher nor author shall be liable for any loss of profit or any other commercial damages, including but not limited to special, incidental, consequential, or other damages.

For general information on our other products and services or for technical support, please contact our Customer Care Department within the United States at (800) 762-2974, outside the United States at (317) 572-3993 or fax (317) 572-4002.

Wiley also publishes its books in a variety of electronic formats. Some content that appears in print may not be available in electronic books. For more information about Wiley products, visit our website at www.wiley.com.

ISBN 978-0-470-94220-8 (cloth); ISBN 978-1-118-06724-6 (ebk); ISBN 978-1-118-06728-4 (ebk); ISBN 978-1-118-06729-1 (ebk)

Printed in the United States of America

10 9 8 7 6 5 4 3 2 1

To Ike, beloved by all

"Bullies cannot exist unless the Employer tacitly permits or encourages bullying behavior."

—Bernice L. Fields

Contents

Foreword

Gary and Ruth Namie are heroes. No one has worked harder, longer, and more successfully to stem the tide of workplace bullying in the United States and beyond. They started with a more general approach with The Work Doctor®, but narrowed their focus some 15 years ago to become the world's leading crusaders against the "jerks, weasels, and snakes" who infect our organizations—and for too many of us—the teams and workgroups that we find ourselves in at this very moment. This book, *The Bully-Free Workplace*, brings together their wisdom, passion, dedication to hard facts, and relentless attention to practical solutions.

Many crusaders become so wrapped up in their goals that they lose the ability to make fact-based decisions and to give valid advice. *The Bully-Free Workplace* does a splendid job of avoiding this problem, bringing the most rigorous evidence available to the table. One of the most difficult problems associated with studying workplace abuse and related topics is that there are so little valid data about prevalence and patterns. We all should be skeptical of web-based surveys that are answered by biased samples, which often reflect a dedication to some political motive rather than to discovering the truth. By far, the most useful and rigorous surveys on bullying have been conducted by the Namies' Workplace Bullying Institute in conjunction with Zogby, a respected survey research firm.

The results of this research are important in many ways, showing, for example, the huge amount of money that workplace bullying costs organizations and the diverse ways in which such abuse damages victims' emotional, physical, and financial well-being.

In particular, these studies provide strong evidence to justify the Namies' focus on organizations and people in positions of power as root causes of workplace bullying. Yes, the Namies show how personality and upbringing can play a role in creating people who are prone to bullying their peers and followers. Yes, they provide detailed and useful advice about how victims can fight against their tormentors. But I believe that the most important and impressive contribution of this useful and compelling book is that it demonstrates that when workplace bullying happens, the organizations where it happens (and the people who have leadership and managerial positions in them) are the primary culprits and even more important, the primary point of intervention for creating bully-free workplaces.

Perhaps the single most important takeaway for me was, as the Namies' advise in Chapter 5, that leaders and organizations ought to start by drawing a firm line in the sand. Drawing a line in the sand, as the Namies show us, is so important because even small incidents of bullying—those little glares and insults, for example—are dangerous signs that more vile and damaging behavior exists or will be tolerated. Once the decision has been made to draw a line in the sand—to me the single most important decision—then both the motivation and logic for building a bully-free workplace start falling into place. Then the range of powerful methods that are proposed and explained here can be applied to each context.

In particular, I urge every boss to study the Namies' list in Chapter 5 of a dozen ways to intervene when bullying incidents happen. Unfortunately, this list runs counter to what happens in most organizations that I know, and if just this set of practices alone were used widely, enormous progress would be made toward building workplaces where jerks, weasels, snakes, and tyrants either change their ways or run for the exits. Consider the Namies' vehement advice: "Do not attempt to put the bully and target across the table from one another to find common ground (mediation) unless the bullying has caused no severe consequences for the target." Yet, time after time, bosses and victims tell me horror stories about the results of forcing victims and their tormentors to "work it out together" even though the victim is terrified of the bully and—especially in the case of smart, powerful, and deluded bullies—such conversations provoke a round of revenge that makes the victim suffer even more.

This is just one small example; *The Bully-Free Workplace* is chock full of other equally useful tips. I especially like how the Namies take considerable pains to show how people in positions of power often do things that unwittingly make it safe for bullies to do their dirty work or, worse yet, are bullies themselves (but are unable or unwilling to admit it to themselves). As I've written elsewhere, especially when people are in power and work under severe pressure, the chances that they will act like assholes and treat people with less power like dirt are quite high. The Namies provide remarkably helpful action steps—developed through their years of practical experience—to help workplace bullies, and those who enable these jerks to do their dirty work, to reverse their vile and destructive ways. I was especially pleased to read that "We've been tough on executives with our candor that they need to stop coddling friends who are bullies. We even invited them to gauge whether or not they are the problem themselves." The next step is for people in power to be as tough on themselves as the Namies are on them!

Finally, not only is the Namies' book well crafted and useful but, as I read it, I realized how much progress this duo has made in the last 15 years (many others have helped, but they've been the most persistent, at least in the United States). They have brought workplace bullying center stage through their writings, proposed legislation, media appearances, expert witnessing, rigorous research, and via so many other ways. As a result, there is now more hope for the victims of bullying than when the authors first started on this crusade. Cynics sometimes suggest to me that it is a waste of time to write and talk about workplace assholes because no matter what anyone does, these jerks will always be with us. The Namies' accomplishments ought to give even the most pessimistic of these cynics cause for optimism. It's a lot harder to get away with being a bully than it used to be. Organizations and their leaders worry about it more than ever before. Victims don't feel alone any longer, and there is an increasingly long and effective list of ways victims can fight back against their tormentors. More than anyone else, we have Gary and Ruth Namie to thank for these improvements. And we have every reason to believe that our workplaces will continue to become more humane as the Namies persist in their crusade and inspire everyone from executives to workers to union leaders to lawmakers to join them on this quest.

—Robert I. Sutton, Stanford Professor
and author of *The No Asshole Rule*

Acknowledgments

Suffolk University Law Professor David Yamada deserves special mention as a partner in the movement for over a decade. His legal treatise in 2000 introduced workplace bullying to the legal lexicon. He is the author of the Healthy Workplace Bill (HWB). David has worked tirelessly in Massachusetts as educator, advocate, and founder of the New Workplace Institute.

Because our work is evidence-driven and research-based, we are indebted to several researchers. Their work is cited throughout the text and in the Notes section. We express thanks to a special few whose work, more than others, informs ours—Peter Schnall, Stale Einarsen, Loraleigh Keashly, Helge Hoel, and Charlotte Rayner.

The legislative campaign is accomplished by a network of volunteer State Coordinators who are the boots on the ground. Every legislative season, they are more successful as amazing citizen lobbyists. When an antibullying law for the workplace is eventually enacted, they deserve the credit. There would be no nationwide campaign without them, and we are grateful.

Our work in organizations is made possible by the countless internal champions who fought uphill battles to bring us into their workplaces. The Waitt Institute for Violence Prevention, Cindy Waitt, director, funded the nation's first Workplace

Bullying in Schools intervention, proving that adults in schools deserve to work in a bullying-free environment, too.

At WBI, we have accomplished small miracles with the help of a too-low-paid staff in recent years—Jessi Brown, Dave Phillips, Noelle Stransky, Carly Morris, and Noel Newell. They accepted jobs but actually serve at the front lines of the national movement. Helping us help organizations implement the Work Doctor® Blueprint program is our team of consultants— Dr. Matt Spencer, Sean Lunsford, Carrie Clark, and Betty Wierda.

This book was a dormant project on a long-postponed "to do list." Wiley editor Lauren Murphy recognized the appropriateness of the timing and prodded us into action. She and editors Christine Moore and Deborah Schindlar have made the book understandable. Renee Maine and Jessi Brown also generously offered editing help.

Preface

Ever since Ruth's experience as a mental health provider in a psychiatry clinic, where she was ravaged by a female supervisor, our lives have been immersed in others' misery. Everyone we have met in the past 14 years since launching the U.S. workplace bullying movement has been touched in some way by bullying. They seem to find us everywhere we go. And although it's certainly been fraught with difficult moments, it's been incredibly uplifting as well.

We've helped the media tell more than 900 heartfelt stories about the plight of individuals bullied at work. We started our work in mid-1997 and hosted a toll-free help line. We heard the stories that flooded our phones in excruciatingly painful detail, one hour at a time. We stopped counting at 6,000 tales. The movement was necessarily framed through the lens of the abused worker. The research done by those of us at the Workplace Bullying Institute (WBI) and our academic colleagues has focused on targets' experiences, because they are the ones readily available for study. Bullied individuals, however, cannot change their employer's practices from the bottom up. It takes leaders within organizations to do that.

We both had had stints as corporate directors in human resources departments in the hospitality and health care industries, which helped to complement our clinical and management professorship roles, respectively. For more than 25 years, we have crafted all kinds of consulting solutions for businesses such as The Work Doctor®. We moved to an exclusive focus on workplace bullying solutions as described in this book when our lives were irreversibly detoured by bullying.

Increased awareness and a future legal mandate have convinced today's employers to finally take action against this timeless, ever-present problem. In 1998, few organizations acknowledged that bullying even existed, let alone took steps to stop it. However, the market is catching up. With the exception of employers in the provinces of Quebec, Saskatchewan, Ontario, and Manitoba, North American employers do not face legal repercussions when they choose to ignore internal reports of bullying. Empirical findings from the WBI national surveys propelled the dialogue about bullying, and denial began to fade. The Healthy Workplace Campaign, which we launched in 2002, has led 18 states to introduce some version of our antibullying legislation. After the senate chambers in both New York and Illinois passed the bill in 2010—only halfway to passage—employer interest in voluntarily controlling bullying rose significantly. We believe that employers are finally ready for this book.

A feature of the best laws, specifically, our Healthy Workplace Bill (HWB), is that the threat of litigation provides the leverage that convinces employers to take voluntary action. The HWB exempts good organizations from liability for the harm caused by abusive employees when those employers develop and establish policy and enforcement procedures as described in this book. So, this book provides the path to compliance with the future law.

Millions of workers who currently suffer at the hands of an abusive boss or coworker will get the relief they deserve when employers understand that it is in their best interests to stop bullying. Only employers can affect the masses—and they shouldn't wait until there is a legal incentive to do so.

Right now, an antibullying advocate in hiding lurks inside every organization. Given the fact that you have purchased this book, chances are that you are that lone person in the organization who has been eager to tackle this issue. You are likely sickened by what you have witnessed. Maybe it has happened to you, and you escaped to safety; or perhaps you were told to identify solutions by a higher-up who cares. In either case, we wrote this book for you, the internal champion. Be aware that you have much alliance building to do before executives willingly endorse a program to stop bullying. We've included a section on mobilizing your organization to focus on the support-building phase of the project. That's the preamble, or the warm-up. Details on exactly what needs to be done—the explicit "how-to" instructions—can be found in the Blueprint.

We love champions. People like you seek our guidance every day. So, we know that we must warn all antibullying advocates: there will be enemies within your organization. They will expend unlimited time and energy to undermine your admirable work and will attempt to defend the abusers' "right" to abuse. Although bullying is a totally irrational and indefensible process, bullying apologists defend their friends with no regard for what is good for the enterprise or public agency. Furthermore, they seem not to care about the detrimental effect on the targeted employee's health. Do not be surprised at how heartless they can be.

Advocates like you are on a moral mission, and unfortunately, capitalism has no morals. Some believe that the modern corporation acts very much like psychopathic individuals. This phenomenon is the conflict that maintains bullying as a routine way of doing business. That is why the forces against you are united and strong; they have the status quo on their side. So gather allies; do not be the lone advocate. Make sure you have a high-ranking friend who is disconnected from the worst bullies. That person—the authentic leader—is the one who can convince others to take action to stop bullying. That leader can take credit for sustaining the organization for the long run.

This book cannot prevent your career assassination. Nevertheless, it is your guide to finding the right leaders for the initiative to purge the jerks, weasels, and snakes from your organization. Welcome to the movement—the employer-based version. Get started today. The task ahead is enormous.

1

Bullies and Bullying

Work is, by its very nature, about violence to the spirit as well as the body. It is, above all (or beneath all), about daily humiliations. To survive the day is triumph enough for the walking wounded among the great many of us.

—Studs Terkel

What's in a Label?

You obviously picked up this book for a reason, and it's likely that one or more jerks, weasels, or snakes works for or with you. It would almost be laughable—that is, if the consequences of their negativity were not so destructive to those they hurt.

What shall we call these perpetrators of organizational chaos? Here are some synonyms for *bullies: aggressors, mobbers, offenders, backstabbers, saboteurs, harassers, nitpickers, control freaks, obsessive critics, terrorists, tyrants, perpetrators*, and *abusers*.

Regardless of the names by which we refer to them, these individuals exhibit conduct far beyond acceptable workplace behavior. They act in non-normative, readily identifiable manners that stand out in extremely negative ways.

The reason you've identified a problem is because you've been able to put a label on the jerk where you work. When you say *weasel*, there is consensus about who fits the description. To call someone a *snake* speaks to the person's deviousness and backstabbing maneuvers.

Throughout this book, we will rely on the simplest of all labels—the bully. It is one we have all lived with since childhood. We shall call all perpetrators, across a wide spectrum of potential negative deeds, bullies. To us, it is no more negative to call someone a bully than it is to brand them using any of the synonyms already suggested. We use the term *bully* as shorthand, not to demonize. To nearly everyone, *bullying* means that something wrong or unacceptable was done—and that we can identify the one who did it.

Nearly all nations recognize the term *bully* or have some cultural variation of it. And believe it or not, the United States is the last among all Western industrialized nations to acknowledge workplace bullying. We're finally joining the rest of the world when we identify the acts of perpetrators of anti-corporate, antiorganizational, and antiworker aggressive actions as bullying.

The power of the term *bully* in the workplace is illustrated by people's reaction when it is used to label them. They usually respond strongly, with instant outrage and denial. They take the label as an insult. Yet it is the bullies themselves—and their deliberate misconduct and nefarious undermining—who insult ethical coworkers who care more about work than workplace politics.

It's Not Just about Bullies

Let's state at the outset that your task is not to identify offenders within your workforce and immediately brand them as bullies. We're not interested in leading you on this kind of witch hunt. Instead, what you will do—if you follow our suggestions in the blueprint—is create a way to identify whoever dares to violate a new, clear set of standards. That person, once detected and con-firmed as a wrongdoer, is referred to as a "policy violator." This is much less pejorative than the label *bully* and a better fit in your (now) bullying-free organization.

There's quite a difference between focusing on bullies and focusing on bully*ing*. Trying to change bullies is a fool's errand. However, if you concentrate on stopping the practice of bully-ing, your leadership quotient will skyrocket, thanks to the grati-tude of so many (currently silent) employees. The first task—to change a bully—falls into the domain of spouses, life partners, and psychiatry. It's not your job to do this for an employee or colleague. Yet it is up to authentic leaders to engineer organiza-tional solutions, and bullying presents ample opportunities to do so.

The Context for Workplace Bullying among other Negative Conduct

Figure 1.1 represents the range of negative behaviors that occur in the workplace—and what can happen as a result of these actions—and places bullying into that continuum. We start on the left, with the least offensive and injurious types of negative behavior, and end on the right, with homicide. Although people who act inappropriately may think they're funny, they frequently say and do stupid things, thus revealing their own lack of knowledge about how to act in public.

Uncivil people violate social norms. They are typically aware of what constitutes "proper" conduct but choose to ignore the limits of acceptability when in the presence of others. They act as though unspoken rules apply to others, but not to them, and they may not feel normative pressure from the group like others do. Working with an uncivil coworker brings rudeness and boorishness—not necessarily aimed at anyone in particular—into your workplace. It's difficult to be a target of incivility because it

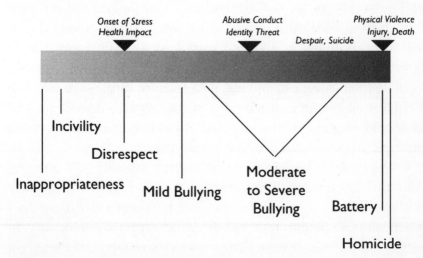

FIGURE 1.1 The Continuum of Negative Interpersonal Behavior

is not personalized. Research by Christine Pearson, the academic most closely identified with the study of incivility, found that only 12 percent of workers subjected to an uncivil workplace *contemplated* leaving. Incivility is only mildly bothersome, hence its location on the continuum.

Disrespect is more hostile and is pointedly aimed directly at another person. It can trigger distress as well as a host of anxiety-related health complications. The perpetrator—the person who's "dissing" another—acts in a manner that shows complete disregard for the target's humanity. It is as if the recipient has not earned the right to be treated well from the perpetrator.

Our experience has found that U.S. employers will tolerate the labels *incivility* or *disrespect* when referring to bullying, whereas Canadian employers are less likely to make euphemistic references to these situations. In other words, Canadian employers are not afraid to refer to bullying as *bullying*.

On the interpersonal behavior scale, mild bullying falls to the right, on the more harsh impact side of disrespect. Mild instances can be covert and infrequent. Bullying becomes moderate to severe when bouts of mistreatment increase in frequency and personalization. Bullies tend to "zone in" on the targeted few, causing their misery to grow exponentially. Compared with incivility, bullying is a laser-focused, systematic campaign of interpersonal destruction—one of warlike dimensions. Methods escalate in abusiveness, and escape routes for targets are blocked. Bullies even recruit coworkers to further spread the misery. And as hatred progresses, the targeted individual grows sicker from multiple stress-related health complications.

Workplace bullying is not merely hostile; it's abusive. And abuse is potentially traumatizing. The result is frequently destabilization—in the form of threats to one's self-identity—when abusers attempt to redefine the target's personality in ways to suit them. It is an extremely invasive tactic. If the target cannot find a way to alleviate the strain, he or she can quickly slide into despair. If hopelessness follows, the person might consider the option of violence.

The National Institutes for Occupational Safety and Health (NIOSH) deemed workplace bullying to be a form of workplace violence. Bullying stops short of physical violence; it is both sublethal and nonphysical. And once in a while, a target turns violent. Violence turned inward is suicide.

Bullying Can Kill Your Organization

Beware how you take away hope from any human being
  —Oliver Wendell Holmes, Jr.

Consider the case of Kevin Morrissey.

In 2010, Morrissey, the managing editor for the *Virginia Quarterly Review*, a literary magazine housed on the campus of the University of Virginia, committed suicide. He left behind the tale of three years of torment at the hands of senior editor Ted Genoways. The university president's office and human resources had known of Morrissey's multiple complaints but had failed to either investigate or suppress Genoways. After his suicide, it was Morrissey's sister who affixed the label of bullying to the case, which caused quite a stir within the academic community across the country.

The provocative nature of the story of Mr. Morrissey's suicide prompted academic writers to recognize bullying in their host institutions.[1] According to the employer's own internal investigation report, the complaints about Genoways were merely "conflicts between a creative, innovative manager and persons who did not share" his views. The employer's report exonerated Genoways. But the campus faced a public relations nightmare for months. The incident undermined the integrity of the *VQR* as well as the university.

When violence is directed outward, it can lead to a work-place homicide, as it did in the following scenario:

On April 16, 2007, Virginia Polytechnic Institute and State University (Virginia Tech) student Seung-Hui Cho, age 23, murdered 32 professors and students and wounded an additional 25. The rational search for an underlying explanation was overshadowed by the round-the-clock media coverage that characterized Cho as a psychopath and walking time bomb. The media revisited the story four months later when the Report of the Virginia Tech Review Panel[2] was delivered to then-governor Kaine. It told of how, during the fall 2005 semester, the introverted Cho was humiliated in front of class-mates by distinguished English professor Nikki Giovanni. She had made repeated demands that his sunglasses be removed and that he participate as the other students did. When Cho didn't respond, Giovanni demanded that Cho leave the class. He didn't do anything, just sat mute; he was terrified to speak, and thus, he was perceived as lazy or rebellious. He was a good writer but feared speaking.

Giovanni, in turn, hysterically threatened to resign unless Cho was removed. Other professors (Robert Hicok and Carl Bean) then had subsequent conflicts with Cho for "being quiet" and graded him accordingly in their classes, giving him a D+. Cho had similar experiences at his housing complex. His scribbling of Romeo's words to Juliet on a door whiteboard to a girl he liked led to misunderstandings, an angry father, and police questioning. The texts of suicidal thoughts that he sent to a suite-mate led him to be involuntarily committed to a psychiatric hospital. After discharge, Cho never received promised psychiatric help. The massive bureaucracy that is Virginia Tech simply lost track of him despite a "Care Team" having the responsibility not to let him disappear.

All of these events preceded the murderous attacks by 15 months. Through official officers—a department chair and several faculty, police, and campus mental health professionals—the university demonized the shy Cho. He remained isolated and untreated up to the time he violently exacted revenge and then killed himself. Ironically, Nikki Giovanni—his original predatory professor—writes fiction that Cho surely must have read as a class assignment. Her poetry contains an excessive amount of violence (Can you kill; Can you piss on a blond head; Can you cut it off; Can you kill; A ni**er can die; We ain't got to prove we can die. We got to prove we can kill.) In a 2006 course for another professor, Cho wrote a story about a character who decides to "kill every god damn person in this damn school" in response to feeling angry and estranged from other students. Was this tragedy preventable?

In the Morrissey and Cho cases, both organizations had ample opportunities to correct the injustice perceived by a person making a complaint and asking for relief from bullying. Both institutions failed to act appropriately and adequately. Two high-publicity negative events rocked those organizations. Thirty-four people died who should not have.

2

Workplace Bullying Defined

A Working Definition

Workplace bullying is the repeated, health-harming mistreatment of an employee by one or more employees through acts of commission or omission manifested as: verbal abuse; behaviors—physical or nonverbal—that are threatening, intimidating, or humiliating; work sabotage, interference with production; exploitation of a vulnerability—physical, social, or psychological; or some combination of one or more categories.

The Workplace Bullying Institute (WBI)

We refer to the recipient of the mistreatment as a targeted—not victimized—worker. To be a target implies temporary mistreatment and abuse with the good likelihood of triumph over the situation when no longer targeted. Conversely, victimhood implies a permanent disruption of normal functioning. Victimhood breeds hopelessness. Perpetrators can be an individual bully acting alone or several acting in collusion.

Bullying at work is easily distinguished from "tough management" by asking "what has this got to do with work?" Bullying will always be used to advance a manager's personal agenda—rendering the target subservient, humiliating a person in front of his team—rather than about getting work done. Bullying actually prevents work from getting done; it's interference. Bullying undermines the government agency's mission and erodes a corporation's profits.

Tough managers are consistently harsh during crunch times. Everyone feels the wrath and mistreatment. Tough, but consistent and fair given the fact that misery is equally distributed, is something workers will tolerate and even respect. The toughness, the abusiveness of bullying, is disproportionately dumped on the targeted few. And there is no end to crunch time. There is no team celebration of a difficult project finished to which the target will be invited.

International Origins

Sweden-based German medical scientist Heinz Leymann founded the international bullying movement, for which he adopted *mobbing* as the name.[3] He borrowed it from the term for many small birds working together to bring down a larger one. For Leymann, it meant a prolonged attack by a group of workers on a single colleague. In Violen, Sweden, he established a government-funded clinic to diagnose and treat workers who suffered "psychological terrorization."[4] Early 1990s research reports from that clinic were the first to link extremely threatening work conditions to posttraumatic stress in workers.

As a result of Leymann's pioneering research and advocacy for workers traumatized by horrific conditions, Sweden enacted the world's first national workplace safety and health ordinance that addressed bullying. The regulations, effective beginning in 1994, called the phenomenon "victimisation at work." In typical Scandinavian fashion, the law focused on protection of workers on the receiving end of "recurrent reprehensible or distinctly negative actions, which are directed against individual employees in an offensive manner. . . . "

Then, in 1992, British BBC radio reporter Andrea Adams, incensed by the abusive treatment of bank workers, became the national spokeswoman for the cause she named "workplace bullying" in her book *Bullying at Work*.[5] She elevated the playground term reserved for children and applied it to adults in their workplaces. After that, bullying of children has been considered as separate from its counterpart: *workplace bullying*.

As far as we're concerned, the only difference between the terms *mobbing* and *bullying* is semantic. Our definition includes situations in which there are both single and multiple perpetrators. There is not one common definition in the field. Again, academics have agreed to disagree and stopped searching for exact wording. However, we all state that bullying is repetitive, uninvited, and overt or covert and that it can lead to some form of personal injury (such as affecting the person's psychological integrity, self-esteem, or health).

Although the United Kingdom does not yet have an omnibus law to address workplace bullying, it does have a 1997/2001 anti-harassment law designed to combat stalking. This criminal law was used successfully against Deutsche Bank in the Helen Green bullying case that awarded the bullied worker $1.5 million.[6] It is a law separate from other statutory laws protecting certain groups from discriminatory mistreatment.

France's "social modernisation" law from 2002 defined *mobbing* as "the perverse implementation of power . . . a means of subjugation and persecution of the other, questioning his fundamental rights as the respect which is due him or her." And speaking of fundamental rights—Germans benefited from a new constitution in the aftermath of World War II—a document that contains the "fundamental rights of persons" wherein bullying is treated as a *constitutional violation*. It turns out that the European economic powerhouse has a higher rate of unionization coupled with better protections for workers' rights than the United States. (See Appendix B and the discussion of macro-bullying trends, of which elimination of unions is one example.)

Ireland enacted a code of practice on the prevention and resolution of workplace bullying that was incorporated into the nation's Safety, Health and Welfare at Work Act in 2005. Bullying is defined there as "repeated inappropriate behaviour, direct or indirect, whether verbal, physical or otherwise, conducted by one or more persons against another or others, at the place of work and/or in the course of employment, which could reasonably be regarded as undermining the individual's right to dignity at work."

Even Australia has several state laws addressing bullying. South Australia's Occupational Safety and Health Code of 2005 goes as far as penalizing employers who ignore *bullying* defined as "behaviour (a) that is directed towards an employee or a group of employees, that is repeated and systematic, and that a reasonable person, having regard to all the circumstances, would expect to victimise, humiliate, undermine or threaten the employee or employees to whom the behaviour is directed; and (b) that creates a risk to health or safety."

The first North American law is the Canadian province of Quebec's Labour Standard (Sec. 81.18) that became effective in June 2004. For legislative purposes, *bullying* is referred to as "psychological harassment at work" with the following definition: "vexatious behaviour that manifests itself in the form of conduct, verbal comments, actions or gestures characterized by the following four criteria: repetitive, hostile or unwanted, affecting the person's dignity or psychological integrity, and resulting in a harmful work environment."

Since May 2008, Canadian federal employees have been protected against bullying under revised provisions of the national Occupational Health and Safety Regulations. Part XX states, "'work place violence' constitutes any action, conduct, threat or gesture of a person towards an employee in their work place including, but not limited to, bullying, teasing, and abusive and other aggressive behaviour, that can reasonably be expected to cause harm, injury or illness to that employee."

In addition to Quebec, three other provinces—Saskatchewan, Ontario, and Manitoba—have enacted health and safety regulatory changes that address workplace bullying as potential health hazards. Manitoba joined the legislative movement, with February 2011 marking the start of employer responsibility to create policies to prevent bullying.

It's clear that Europeans and Canadians treat the psychological integrity and dignity of persons quite seriously. We believe that American disregard for such factors—by often discounting employees as "whiny" or "too soft"—says less about the European perspective than about the mythology of American toughness. Human susceptibility to stress-related diseases is unrelated to geography.

At present, there's not a single U.S. state with a law or a provision in an occupational safety and health code that deals with workplace bullying. You can read about the status of multiple versions of the antibullying Healthy Workplace Bill that have been introduced since 2003 at the website for the Healthy Workplace Campaign (healthyworkplacebill.org). The definition of an abusive work environment in the legislation is the WBI definition of workplace bullying.

National Prevalence

WBI conducted the only two large-scale scientific surveys of workplace bullying in the United States: the first in 2007 and the second in 2010. The complete results of these surveys and other work by the authors can be found in Appendix B. The polls were considered "scientific" because Zogby International randomly sampled a group of adult Americans for us. Both national surveys used the previous WBI definition of workplace bullying without actually referencing the term *workplace bullying* in the survey item.

At the time of the summer 2010 survey, approximately 153 million Americans were working. Nine percent of the population—or 13.7 million Americans—confessed to currently being bullied, and an additional 26 percent had been bullied previously but were not enduring such mistreatment at the time. A separate group, accounting for 15 percent of the respondents, had witnessed the bullying of coworkers but had never personally experienced it. These results indicate that half of adult Americans were familiar with bullying, either directly or vicariously. The remaining half of the population reported that they had never seen or personally experienced bullying. For this group, bullying is out of sight, out of mind.

Women make up a slight majority (57 percent) of targeted individuals, and most bullies are men (62 percent). Male bullies tend to target other men slightly more frequently (56 percent) than they do women (46 percent). Female bullies (38 percent of the population) target women significantly more (80 percent) than they target men (20 percent). In the section on managers' and supervisors' preparation, we will discuss the special case of women managers targeting other women. Most bullying (68 percent) is same-gender mistreatment.

Rank is quite clearly related to bullying; the stereotype of a bullying boss is not a myth. According to the 2007 WBI U.S. Workplace Bullying Survey, bullies are bosses (who outrank their targets by at least one level in the organizational chart) 72 percent of the time. Coworkers account for 18 percent of the bullies, and the remaining 10 percent manage to bully up the corporate ladder from subordinate roles.

Tactics Used by Bullies

There is no character, howsoever good and fine, but it can be destroyed by ridicule, howsoever poor and witless.
—Mark Twain

In 2003, WBI conducted an online survey of 1,300 website visitors. This nonscientific sample provided a glimpse of the work world through a bullied individual's eyes. Bullies most commonly adopted 15 tactics. In descending order from most to least frequent, they are as follows:

1. Falsely accuse someone of "errors" not actually made
2. Stare, glare, be nonverbally intimidating and show clear signs of hostility
3. Discount the person's thoughts or feelings ("Oh, that's silly") in meetings
4. Use the "silent treatment" to "ice out" and ostracize others
5. Exhibit presumably uncontrollable mood swings in front of the group
6. Make up his or her own rules on the fly that even the bully did not follow
7. Disregard satisfactory or exemplary quality of completed work despite evidence
8. Harshly and constantly criticize having a different "standard" for the target
9. Start, or fail to stop, destructive rumors or gossip about the person
10. Encourage others to turn against the person being tormented
11. Single out and isolate one person from coworkers, either socially or physically
12. Publicly display "gross," undignified (but not illegal) behavior
13. Yell, scream, or throw tantrums in front of others to humiliate a person
14. Steal credit for work done by others
15. Abuse the evaluation process by lying about the target's performance

The Negative Acts Questionnaire (NAQ) is a checklist that academic researchers use to define bullying.[7] In this context, bullying is said to have occurred when a person reports that at least two acts are experienced weekly for at least six continuous months. Here's a sample of the NAQ items. You have been bullied if you

- had information withheld that affected your performance;
- were ordered to do work below your level of competence;
- were reminded repeatedly of your errors or mistakes;
- were humiliated or ridiculed in connection with your work;
- received hints or signals from others that you should quit your job;
- had key tasks removed and replaced with trivial, unpleasant tasks;
- had false allegations made against you;
- were subjected to excessive teasing and sarcasm;
- had been shouted at or targeted with spontaneous anger or rage.

Our academic colleague Pam Lutgen-Sandvik used the NAQ in a study where she also asked participants if they believed they had been bullied.[8] According to the responses, 28 percent had met the criteria and were categorized as bullied targets. In contrast, only 9.2 percent of participants defined themselves as bullied. This is a reliably replicated finding.

Objective classification rates are higher than rates at which people will admit they were targets of bullying themselves. They are reluctant because of the stigma associated with victimhood. The stigma is part shame (feelings of worthlessness, believing the lies about personal incompetence) and part guilt (for having allowed someone to meddle in one's life so much). The finding also shows that bullied targets are not whiners or complainers. They are exactly the opposite—stoic and proud.

3

Impact on Targeted Employees

Health Harm

We experience positive stress, referred to as *eustress*, when completing challenging work or physical or mental exercise. Although this kind of effort taxes the body, it produces desirable activities. The opposite of this—the destructive side of stress—is known as *distress*. Factors do exist that can minimize the harmful effects of stress on the body. These include predictability of negative events, actual or illusory control over one's fate, and availability of validating social support from friends and family. There is also a danger of physical health impairment from prolonged exposure to safety-threatening environmental factors known as stressors. External to the person, stressors trigger the biological human stress response that is the marvelously coordinated activation of the nervous system and secretion of hormones that affect both the body and brain. Harm from bullying—and the direct physical response we experience—can be traced to stress.

Bullying at work has been repeatedly linked to cardiovascular and gastrointestinal diseases. Although symptoms aren't obvious, hypertension is the first warning sign. Targets may suffer ischemia (a restriction in blood supply), strokes, heart attacks, and cardiac failure. Dr. Peter Schnall and other occupational health researchers have been conducting 30-year longitudinal studies that correlate job strain with coronary heart disease.[9] Job strain is the simultaneous increase of task demand—such as quantity, quality, or rate of production—combined with decreased personal control over outcomes in the form of abusive supervision or exclusion from collaborative decision making. The primary stress-related gastrointestinal problem is irritable bowel syndrome, followed by conditions such as chronic fatigue, fibromyalgia, and some skin disorders that can be worsened by stress as well. According to Robert Sapolsky, the Stanford University stress guru,[10] it is not stress itself that kills but stress-related *diseases.*

Stress at work may very well be taking years off your life. The 2009 Nobel Prize winner in Medicine and Physiology, Elizabeth Blackburn, demonstrated that stress even interferes with the process of cellular replication. Blackburn discovered that telomeres—the structures that protect DNA chromosomes ensuring the ability to replicate—are destroyed by prolonged stress. Telomere destruction results in shortened life spans. The average number of years lost for women varied from as much as 9 to 12 years in one study.[11]

Thanks to advances in neuroscience measurement of brain activity, researchers can now show how social exclusion and hurling insulting epithets actually trigger pain.[12] There is also evidence that areas of the brain that are essential for memory and emotional regulation can shrink and lose capacity to perform when stress continues.[13]

Emotional health is also compromised when stress is unremitting. In a 1990 scientific journal publication,[14] Heinz Leymann showed that prolonged exposure to mobbing—aka, bullying at work—actually triggers posttraumatic stress disorder (PTSD) in recipients. Respondents in the WBI 2003 online survey of bullied targets reported that 30 percent of women and 21 percent of men were diagnosed with PTSD. Research by Stale Einarsen compared PTSD generated by workplace stressors with PTSD caused by nonworkplace events.[15] He and his colleagues found that work trauma is as severely emotionally damaging as rape. Other studies draw connections between the mental health consequences of being sexually harassed and being bullied—except that bullying causes more depression, anger, and hostility.[16] Our own studies found that nearly every bullied worker experiences overwhelming anxiety, and clinical depression afflicts nearly 40 percent of targets.

Disrupted Social Lives

Coworkers resent being involuntarily dragged into another person's misery, vicarious bullying. Even if they don't directly witness the misconduct, everyone knows what happened when the target emerges from a closed-door session with the bully. The slumped shoulders and defeated looks are painful to see. And the personal discomfort and realistic fear that they could be next combine to convince witnesses to isolate and eventually even abandon their colleagues.

Stress that bullied targets bring home affects their children and spouses in the form of displaced anger. Parents also transmit subtle cues about their own distress, and bullying prevents them from being emotionally present during their children's development. Neurological evidence suggests that if this kind of detachment continues unabated, neglected children can experience inadequate mental growth. The connection between misery brought home from a toxic workplace—and its effects on childhood bullying and aggression (due to complex child trauma)—is the topic of new research.

Coworkers sometimes voluntarily "ice out" their friends (tactic 4 in the list of tactics used by bullies) and can be easily persuaded to betray their colleagues at the bully's request or command (tactic 10). Excluding colleagues from the group's social life is surprisingly painful. Ostracism is a severe punishment for humans, who require social support to fend off destructive stress—and this type of isolation magnifies stress's already detrimental effects.

Although family and friends offer support for longer periods than coworkers, even they can tire—and bullying often lasts months or years. Observers want the target to break free but blame him or her for staying if no solution is forthcoming. A 2000 WBI study revealed that female partners stayed with their bullied mates longer than men partners stayed with women mates. Divorces and breakups are common in marriages in which one partner is bullied at work.

Economic Harm

Loss of professional status affects income by way of denied opportunities—promotions given to others, demotions used as punishment, and rejection of earned vacation as well as other forms of paid time off. Bullied targets routinely lose status as they fall out of favor with bullying managers. The ultimate impact is job loss for no cause—an abuse of managerial prerogative.

The 2010 WBI U.S. Workplace Bullying Survey found that 41 percent of bullied women and 36 percent of bullied men quit their jobs. The responses tell us that they had not considered quitting before being bullied. The survey was conducted during one of the toughest economic times for American workers; nearly 10 percent of Americans had registered as unemployed, and approximately 18 percent of included respondents were not working or were underemployed. In other words, it was a time during which *no one* would want to quit if it was avoidable. Bullying almost always forced targets to choose between two equally unattractive alternatives. Involuntary job loss was the second most frequent result. An additional 25 percent of the women and 13 percent of the men were terminated subsequent to being bullied. In 2010, approximately 2.9 million Americans could blame their job loss on bullying.[17]

From a corporate executive's viewpoint, workers have no right to expect job security—a point with which we completely agree. However, when rogue managers arbitrarily displace quality, hard workers simply to prove that they have the power to ruin another person's livelihood, it is wrong. And they can easily camouflage this with simultaneous, massive layoffs.

4

How Bullying Kills Good Organizations Like Yours

Although the term *killing* might sound somewhat melodramatic, Heinz Leymann minced no words in describing mobbing as psychological terrorization. *Social misery* was one of the gentler synonyms he also used. Leymann even titled one of his books *The Suicide Factory*.[18] He suggested that tyrannical behavior—the kind that can drive an adult to suicide—is strongly toxic. Abusive work environments that cause employees deep distress are not trivial matters, and preventable stress-related diseases *do* kill people. Here are some bad things that could be happening to your good organization if bullying has taken hold.

Unaddressed Bullying Exposes the Organization to the Risk of Violence

The documentary *Murder By Proxy: How America Went Postal* was released in 2010.[19] Experts in the film analyze the background stories of several workplace massacres. Although it does not excuse the shootings or the murders, experts all cite work conditions prior to the event that organization leaders clearly should have noticed. Warning signs were present in almost every single case. Troubled, toxic workplaces are potentially incendiary sites where violence can explode with lethal force. For example, prior to the fateful November 14, 1991, massacre at Royal Oak, Michigan, by Thomas McIlvaine—who killed five, including himself—there was a systematic campaign of intimidation and humiliation by a team of postal managers new to Royal Oak. They tormented the employee who loved his job and happened to be a "tough guy" because he fought in martial arts, stood up to abusive managers, and was a Marine Corps veteran. Fifteen months passed from the time of his termination as a result of a manufactured charge of "insubordination" to the time of the massacre. The film's message is straightforward and unquestionable: these horrific consequences were indeed preventable.

The "going postal" incidents, each with a deeper, more complex story behind the gruesome headlines, all suggested that there were warning signs ignored by the employer. The previously discussed cases at the University of Virginia and Virginia Tech illustrated the point that some red flags appeared but they were ignored.

Turnover of the Wrong People

Unfortunately, it's the best and brightest—not the expendable dullards—who are frequently chased away. Most are driven out by conditions made deliberately so unbearable that no one could stay; this is known as constructive discharge. Others quit for reasons directly tied to the unremitting stress from bullying managers. The banished are the workers who threaten their managers. From our 2003 online survey, we identified the top four reasons given by targets for their selection by bullies. The most frequent reason given was "independence," their refusal to be or act subservient. Factors two and three were about posing a threat—more technical competence in the job than the bully and better liked by customers and coworkers. The fourth ranked factor was being ethical and honest and willing to expose fraud (to be a whistleblower). Company executives rarely learn about the numerous, expensive sacrifices unless the targets also operate at, or near, the top levels.

Turnover Rates Are Uneven across Units

Your marketplace competitiveness is only as strong as the weakest unit. Just because some are spared doesn't mean that no problem exists. Workers in units where bullies operate are hit hard.

Transfer requests abound. Headhunters are circling like buzzards. Good people want out. The losses in distressed units remain invisible to all but the most inquisitive and detail-oriented executives because some people make it their jobs to hide the truth.

Bullies Expose the Organization to Litigation Risk

At a cardiac treatment center in Indiana in 2001, former chief perfusionist Joe Doescher sued cardiologist Dr. Dan Raess for damages after he left his job due to emotional distress. According to evidence presented at the trial, Raess verbally assaulted Doescher and charged toward him with a clenched fist. The civil jury, believing that Doescher felt sufficiently threatened by Raess's conduct, found Raess guilty of assault and awarded $325,000 to Doescher.

The trial was dubbed the nation's first "bullying trial" because this book's first author testified as an expert witness and was called on to declare Raess a bully. Although this verdict was reversed by an appellate court in 2005, the Indiana Supreme Court overturned that reversal and reinstated the award in 2008.[20] Part of the Supreme Court opinion confirmed the reality of workplace bullying and suggested it can indeed be the cause of emotional distress.

As another example, consider the 2005 lawsuit filed by two former employees at City University of New York—Gloria Salerno, PhD, and Emelise Aleandri, PhD—against the university; the plaintiffs shared a $1.4 million settlement in that case.[21] Joseph Scelsa, the director of CUNY's Calandra Italian-American Institute, subjected the two to humiliation, demotions, and career-threatening decisions. Scelsa stripped licensed clinical psychologist Salerno of her student counseling duties. Aleandri, producer and host of a successful CUNY TV show *Italics*, lost her job to a former script typist for the show and mistress of the married Scelsa.

Disability Costs Rise

One disability management (return-to-work) company with which we partnered estimated that 18 percent of all claims were based on psychological stress attributable to workplace bullying.[22] The majority of claims were based on a bullying boss. The average number of days bullied targets missed per claim was 159, which equals *a lot* of lost productivity.

Absenteeism/Presenteeism

Bullied targets use all of their paid time off—and then some. At first, they take mental health days. But as the bullying lingers or escalates, workers lose the ability to come to work daily. Collaborative projects are suspended while the key employee is off sick. Those with the strongest and proudest work ethic find it impossible to stay at work in the toxic work environment.

Presenteeism refers to workers coming to work sick. They underperform and tend to infect coworkers with viruses. In America, missing work is often grounds for termination by unforgiving employers. So, people refuse to miss work when they should. A second, more devious form of presenteeism is when the worker is physically onsite but is disengaged. Time at work is spent sending out resumes for the next good job or sabotaging the current employer to retaliate for some perceived injustice.

Intangible Costs for Good Employers

Bullies tarnish your organization's reputation within professional groups, making it harder to recruit hard-to-find professionals. You slip from the pantheon of "Great Places to Work"[23] to one of the "Worst Places." Eventually, it's almost impossible to launch any new initiatives that require employee trust or loyalty—because both were eroded as the bully gutted one department after another while nothing was done. All new ventures are greeted with employee cynicism, resentment, or indifference. Staff members are generally unengaged due to the broken psychological contract between you and them. They expected to be kept safe but were assaulted by one or more bullies who acted without fear of consequences—and in their opinion, you are the one who let this abuse continue and failed to protect them.

Is It an Epidemic?

We know from the 2010 WBI U.S. Workplace Bullying Survey that *13.7 million adult Americans are currently being bullied.* In 2006, the United Nation's International Labour Organization (ILO) declared that violence at work, ranging from bullying and mobbing to sexual harassment to homicide, was reaching epidemic levels.[24] According to the ILO, in 2002, there were 800,000 mobbing (bullying) victims in Germany, and 22 percent of public officials in Spain report being mobbed.

The epidemic, however, is a hidden one. The targeted workers suffer mostly in shame and silence, and issues of legality render much of the abuse covert. Without formal complaints of policy violations, the organization can operate as if the bullying never happens. Policies are typically crafted to comply with legislative mandates. Without laws, bullying policies in the workplace are not required. All of these factors combine to render bullying an "undiscussable" topic in contemporary organizations.

Still Legal in the United States after All These Years

This is difficult for the public to understand. Most bullying is legal—and here's why: the belief is that a "hostile work environment," sexual harassment, and racial discrimination are all illegal for everyone. The truth is that seeking a legal solution to those three problems is restricted to victims who enjoy membership in a protected status group—women, people older than age 40, people with disabilities, or those with strong religious views. That is what proving discrimination requires. You have to be able to show that you were treated differently (or, to use the legal term, *disparately*) because you were a woman or older than age 40 or a member of one of the other protected groups.

The tricky part occurs if your harasser is also protected, in which case, the victim might not have a claim. When harasser and victim are of the same gender, age, or race, violations of laws are nearly impossible. The law, for example, does not cover woman-on-woman harassment. In fact, we know from the national 2007 WBI U.S. Workplace Bullying Survey that illegal discrimination happens in only 20 percent of cases of mistreatment. That means that the vast majority of situations are bullying. And although they are harmful and debilitating, they are not legally actionable.

Employer policies are designed to comply with federal and state laws governing discriminatory misconduct. If certain conduct is illegal, then there will be an internal policy to prohibit it. Similarly, if state or federal laws do not address misconduct, employers need not create policies to prohibit it. That's why so few employers do anything about bullying.

And that's also why *you* are a pioneering employer. Your organization wants to address workplace bullying voluntarily. You are not waiting for a law to declare it illegal. It is wreaking havoc in your workplace—so you have decided to act now.

5

An Illustrative Case

Background

Kate, age 48, started working as an assistant technician when she was 21. Her past 14 years of work have been with a large insurer. Kate, working directly under the vice president, is one in a six-person team of highly creative, highly educated people.

The team is responsible for critical projects requiring sophisticated mathematical modeling to predict risk exposure for the firm. The team was well known for its history of technical collaboration and spontaneous social support for one another.

The Start

Things began to change for Kate when the vice president she worked for left the company to take a job elsewhere. Instead of conducting a thorough search for a new vice president, the senior vice president brought in his former coworker from a competing firm.

Irena, age 44, was hired. She had a marketing background and no technical or mathematical experience. She had also worked for the senior vice president who hired her at another company.

Kate's team was notified two days before Irena's arrival. At that time, they were also told that there was a shakedown occurring in the company. Irena's job was to "whip" their team into shape. They were to beat their overseas counterpart division or risk the dissolution of the entire team and the loss of all their jobs. The team was devastated to learn that they were to do this with a new director who did not have the skills needed to help them with their technical work.

Month 1

Irena spent most of her time in meetings with the executive team of directors. These meetings were traditionally open to all, but with Irena in attendance, the meetings were kept closed. She held only weekly meetings with the team and private sessions with some members of the team; she never met privately with Kate. Team members never knew what was going on, and time and money were lost.

Target Selection

Irena saw that Kate was the quietest at meetings. Kate was naturally quiet and liked to listen before she spoke. Irena also saw that Kate was the one that others seemed to rely on for information. Kate was nurturing to colleagues.

Behind closed doors in the first private session, Irena told Kate of her suspicions that Kate was undermining her. She told Kate that she was "watching her" and didn't like how much time she spent with other workers. Kate began to explain, but Irena cut her off. She obviously did not want a two-way conversation. Irena spent the rest of the hour describing her management style to Kate.

Ambush

In subsequent team meetings, Irena solicited contributions from the team, giving the appearance that decisions would be consultative and that she would incorporate input from everyone. Whenever Kate contributed (after raising her hand to get permission to speak, which she felt instinctively she had to), Irena ridiculed her with discounting and sarcastic comments such as, "I expected more from you than that" and "Of course. Isn't that obvious to anyone with half a brain?" Kate was dumbfounded and embarrassed. She had never been treated like this at this company, or anywhere else for that matter.

Kate's peers were supportive but only in private. After meetings, they commented to Kate, "Hang in there" and "Wait to see what Irena wants before speaking up next time; don't let her fluster you." When Kate asked them if they would help her, they all said they didn't want to become involved in fear that Irena might target them.

Month 2

Irena intensifies the trouble she causes Kate. In the beginning, there was always some ambiguity that allowed Kate to try to discount what was being done to her. In Month 2, Irena becomes very clear. Kate's uncertainty fades.

Formalizing the Campaign of Interpersonal Destruction
Irena began weekly private meetings with Kate. Described as "work sessions," in reality they were specific times set aside and used to shake Kate's confidence in her very real competence. Irena would say things like, "I can't be specific now, but I sense that whatever skills you once had are slipping." Kate couldn't reply. Her jaw dropped.

A Destabilizing Pattern: Strain-Respite-Strain
Irena took every opportunity to humiliate Kate at team meetings. There were two consecutive weekly sessions during the second month when Irena inexplicably withheld her excessive criticism typically disproportionately dumped on only Kate. For two weeks, Kate believed her crisis had passed. She felt relaxed at work for the first time since her first meeting with Irena. But the peace lasted only two weeks. Then, Irena resumed the campaign against Kate.

Physical Symptoms
Kate began to experience a feeling of general malaise. She was confused. She worried that she had done something wrong. At

work, she strove to work harder and longer, skipping lunches. She wanted to prove Irena wrong. Kate never shared Irena's accusations with her friends on the team. She was not yet certain what was happening, but this was the beginning of stress.

At home, Kate's husband told her to stand up to Irena. He felt that if she stood her ground, Irena would act like any normal person and see what a good and valuable worker Kate was. Kate had never encountered someone who had worked against the company. She had no idea how to fight back. She had not been assaulted and bushwhacked like this before. She was the proverbial "deer in the headlights," historically composed and competent, now suddenly helpless and clueless.

Months 3 to 5

Health harm can have a delayed onset. Emotional trauma, for instance, can take weeks or months to materialize. Though blood pressure is a relatively quick indicator of physical stress, because there are so few warning signs, people do not have it diagnosed until much later.

Physical Stress

Kate began to feel physically ill. She had frequent headaches, stomachaches, and fatigue. One day, Kate took a half day of her paid time off to visit her family physician. Kate did not share the situation at work with the doctor, nor did he bother to ask. He did find, however, that she had high blood pressure and irritable bowel syndrome. The connection between Irena's actions directed against Kate and these symptoms were missed. These were all the beginnings of diseases brought on by stress.

In addition, Kate's nights were sleepless. Every night's conversation with her husband was obsessing over Irena, specifically why Irena was doing this to Kate. Fatigue, not lack of intelligence, made it impossible for her to concentrate at work. Her mood grew gloomier each day.

Divide and Conquer, Group Abandonment

Irena called an impromptu meeting with the other directors. She told them that she was "concerned about" Kate's apparently failing performance. Irena hinted strongly that the former, too lenient vice president had "obviously overrated" Kate. Team members stared at one another but remained silent. No one dared mentioned Irena's one-woman campaign against Kate, and no one told Kate about the meeting staged behind her back.

After the secret meeting, two of the team members who were originally closest to Kate stopped spending free time at the office with her. No one lunched with her. Coworkers invented various reasons to cancel off-work social time with Kate and her spouse that they used to routinely enjoy. Kate felt isolated from the once-close team at work and social activities outside work.

Month 6

Targets like Kate wait a long time (the stigma of personal shame or guilt) to ask the employer for help. When they eventually do ask for relief, they expect positive results. The troubles experienced prior to engaging the employer pale in comparison with the troubles about to be experienced.

Human Resource Response

Kate turned to a long-time acquaintance in the human resource (HR) department, Susie. Kate asked Susie if she, Kate, was "crazy." Susie confirmed that Kate had always been an exemplary, citation-winning employee, so, no, Kate was not crazy. Kate asked how to deal with Irena. With Kate's question, Susie grew colder and said that it was Kate's responsibility to fix the problem and to get along with her boss. Susie suggested that Kate take Irena to lunch to get to know her. That way, Kate could learn what it is that Irena would like Kate to change. Kate could then ask Irena to help her become that person. The HR message was that Irena was boss. Kate had to adjust. Irena was entitled to act as she chose with impunity.

Attempted Resolution-Confrontation

In the following weeks, Kate tried to follow the HR message by trying to schedule a meeting with Irena. This attempt proved unsuccessful. Kate, however, moved forward with her plan and prepared the agenda for the meeting. She planned to be rational and appeal to Irena's need to best utilize Kate's demonstrable technical skills to help the team get on track. There had simply been a misunderstanding between Irena and Kate, an awkward start to a new relationship. Repair was possible if both Kate and Irena were willing to work at it. Kate believed that Irena, wanting to be seen as a good manager, would listen and want to cooperate. This was the meeting Kate rehearsed every night at home with her husband.

The meeting was finally scheduled. At the start, Kate blurted out how badly she was made to feel by Irena. She started to read her list, but the meeting took a very different turn. Irena admonished Kate not to blame her, to look inward, and to take personal responsibility as an adult.

It turned out Irena was also prepared. She rattled off a list of Kate's performance "problems" and "inappropriate incidents," the descriptions of which were vague. There was no quantifiable or measurable evidence. Kate never had a chance to point out her skills and what she could do to make their relationship work for the company.

Irena alluded to only her "gut feeling" as the source of her accusations. Irena revealed that the HR director (Susie's boss) instructed her to create a performance improvement plan (PIP) for Kate. This meant Kate's tenure was suspended. She was placed on 90-day probation requiring intense scrutiny and monitoring. Without improvement, as judged by Irena, Kate faced termination. Irena also made the point that the senior vice president with whom Kate always got along was now siding with Irena.

To make things worse, the next day, Irena ordered Kate to keep a daily record of time spent on every task and personal time, including bathroom breaks and meals. Kate had to submit the record every day to Irena's assistant.

A Legal Lesson about Harassment
After this, Kate returned to HR to file a complaint against Irena. The Equal Employment Opportunity (EEO) discrimination officer told her that since both parties are women of approximately the same age and race, there really is no law to prohibit what Kate considers "harassment." Since both are women and members of "legally protected classes" (both women, both older than 40), Irena's misconduct does not violate any legal standard. Company policies, Kate learned, follow state and federal laws. The woman told Kate, "There are no laws against being an asshole or committing cruelty, short of physical violence in the workplace."

Stress Escalates
Once more Kate visited her physician. This time he noted the dangerous rise in her blood pressure and her apparent anxiety at work, as evidenced by Kate not being able to catch her breath. All of this was in addition to Kate's sense of dread from the simple act of driving to work. This time, he wrote an off-work order for five working days to give Kate a break from the stressful routine. He also counseled her to find another job quickly because "this one will kill you."

Arbitrary and Capricious Rule Changing
Kate dreaded the return to work but did not consider staying away. On her first day back, before Kate could check in with her

team, Irena called Kate into her office. She was chastised for taking time off work and told that her deadline for improvement (originally 90 days) was shortened to 45 days. Irena repeated the threat of looming termination.

Kate had a panic attack on site. She barely made it out of Irena's office to call her physician. He told her to go to the hospital emergency room. One of her colleagues called her husband to transport her. As Kate sat helpless in a chair, Irena stood in her open office door and leered. Later, the emergency room doctor wrote a two-week off-work order for job stress. The document was faxed to Irena.

Clueless Counselors, Secondary Bullying

On leave, Kate called the company employee assistance program (EAP) for a referral to a mental health counselor. At the appointment, the therapist was kind but refused to advise Kate on how to handle Irena. The therapist characterized Irena as an "admittedly difficult person with which to deal." The therapist then explained that this was not what EAP was about and added that EAP worked best when the limited time away from work was spent on matters in Kate's control, not workplace issues. The three allotted sessions were meant to examine what about Kate triggered Irena's wrath and how Kate needed to change to mitigate the triggers. The plan sounded good at first, but by the time Kate arrived home, she had grown infuriated at the notion that she was the one supposed to change. She had done nothing, and it was a gross injustice that Irena could not be made to change her behavior toward Kate!

A Turning Point

Irena sent an e-mail to Kate at home suggesting that Kate consider quitting the company if she lacked the stamina to work for her. Kate printed the message and started a file, not sure how, or if, it would ever be used. The e-mail was the last straw for Kate's husband. He had watched his wife come home verbally beaten and abused, and he could no longer support any efforts to try and appease Irena. He supported his wife and her decision to quit.

Journey toward Discovery Begins

Kate called her daughter living across the country. She advised her mother to tell the chief executive officer (CEO) about abusive Irena. Kate asked her daughter if using the term *abusive* was too strong. The daughter asked Kate if she felt as if she had been abused. The daughter then told her mom about discovering workplace bullying. Late that night, Kate spent hours online, recognizing for the first time that she did not invite the mistreatment. Kate now had a name for what had happened to her. She learned to contrast it with illegal harassment.

While on sick leave, Kate called HR, inquiring about using time off. She was put on hold until her friend in HR, Susie, came on the line and advised her of the only options: (1) take unpaid Family Medical Leave Act (FMLA) time, (2) file a workers' compensation claim and wait 6 to 10 months for a decision, or (3) quit. Kate felt abandoned by the company.

The Final Ambush

At the end of the two-week leave, Kate returned to work, demoralized and as thoroughly "disengaged" as an employee could be. Although she had loved her company and her work, she felt as though she was being watched and found it hard to work. Her worst fears were realized when Irena found her 10 minutes before lunch and called her into the conference room.

Seated around the conference table were the senior vice president, Susie from HR, and Irena. Since Kate was not a member of a union, she was alone (and didn't even think to ask someone to accompany her). Irena told her that given the frequency of sick time, Kate was becoming a burden to her colleagues. Irena said that several employees had complained to her. Thus,

Kate's "erratic and unpredictable behavior" compelled Irena to let her go.

Kate would have one month's severance pay and employer-paid health care insurance for that period. Irena told Kate to sign the prepared agreement that stated Kate had chosen to voluntarily leave the company and forever forfeited the right to pursue litigation of any kind against the company (this also applied to her family, heirs, and successors). No one else spoke. Kate then addressed Susie and asked, "How is this fair when I've done nothing wrong, ever, in my 14 years here?" Susie replied, "This is the best solution for everyone." Kate signed and shrugged in resignation. Irena was the first to leave the room. Susie gathered the papers and left.

The Perp Walk

Outside the door waited a security guard. Susie and the guard escorted Kate to her desk. They waited while she filled a box with personal belongings from a 14-year career in the department. She was made to surrender her security badge and keys, told not to touch the computer (it is, after all, company property), and escorted to her car by the guard.

Immediate Aftermath

Kate felt degraded by the escorted removal from the workplace. She had an overwhelming sense of injustice over the entire scenario. When she called former colleagues, they didn't answer. When she attempted to reach them at work, they whispered that they were told not to talk to her at any time and hung up.

1 Month after Leaving

Kate applied for unemployment. To her surprise, she was denied because she had voluntarily quit according to the employer's response to the claim. Officially she had, but she felt she had been coerced. She had no witnesses and she had signed the agreement.

When health insurance stopped, she was offered an extension (COBRA), but the unemployed Kate could not afford the $1,200 monthly premium. She priced insurance coverage for individuals with a broker, and the rate dropped to $700 per month. The problem was that all carriers stipulated that she had a preexisting "mental illness" because of the depression induced by Irena and noted in her medical records. At a time when Kate was most at risk and needed health care, it was not available to her.

For the Company

Irena recruited and hired a man younger than Kate as her replacement. His starting compensation was the same as Kate's final rate, despite him having less education and experience. Irena told him and anyone who asked that the position had been vacant because a less competent worker was let go. Irena, working with the company only six months before chasing out Kate, became the oral historian with the ability to mischaracterize the extensive contributions Kate had made over the years. The memory of Kate was effectively erased. Coworkers familiar with the truth were too afraid to counter Irena lest they suffer the same fate as Kate.

The senior vice president had his former colleague Irena by his side, and he was very happy.

The HR director and Susie had served the senior vice president and Irena well. They continued to assist Irena in any way she asked.

6 Months after Leaving

Kate's depression worsened, and her physician referred her to a psychiatrist. Medications were prescribed. The company-paid health insurance was set to end in a couple of weeks, and she was afraid she would not be able to afford the treatment she needed because her husband's company did not offer insurance to him or her.

Losing Kate's income made mortgage payments more difficult. Kate had finally started looking for work as her energy slowly returned. She tried to use her former vice president as a reference, but recruiters all asked for the name of her most recent supervisor. With Irena as a reference, Kate was not invited for interviews. One kind reference checker told Kate that Irena had described Kate to her as irresponsible. Irena had said that Kate was let go for problems with her stamina and social relations.

Kate, now 49, is still looking for meaningful professional work.

6

Why Bullies Bully

Bullies are always cowards at heart and may be credited with a pretty safe instinct in scenting their prey.

—Anna Julia Cooper

We think it's safe to assume that your purchase of this book shows your interest in stopping workplace bullying. Along with that interest must come some curiosity. You wouldn't be human if you didn't wonder why bullies act as they do. But be warned, if you spend too much time ruminating about the bully's motivation, you can get stuck on a pet theory or two and never actually take any steps to stop the bullying. Are you in the business of theory building or leading a world-class organization?

We offer this chapter to help you understand the variety of sources of bullying. First, we cover some fun explanations. Then, we offer our three-part model about why bullying occurs in your workplace, and we lead you to actionable steps to stop it. By the end of this chapter, you will know enough about the "why" to move on to the "what to do."

Causes That Cannot Be Corrected

Let's begin with some explanations about the causes of bullying that are certainly true. They are true explanations, but keep in mind that these do little to rid the workplace of bullies.

Biology and Early Life Experiences

For starters, consider the brain of a hyperaggressive bully. He or she may have a too tiny prefrontal cortex to enable her or him to control impulses. This makes the person quick to become angry and quick to bully. However, unless you're prepared to lobotomize these people, it's just a fun fact to know with no action possible on your part.

Another explanation for a certain proportion of bullies is that they were abused in their families of origin. They grew up either witnessing domestic violence or being the personal target of abuse or violence by a parent or relative. From that chaotic, messed up way of dealing with personal conflict and differences comes a very distorted adult perspective on how to deal with life. Of course, not everyone who is abused becomes an abuser. Not everyone repeats the cycle of violence. And even though abuse is a legitimate basis for some people's aggression, there's nothing you can do as a manager or leader about reengineering someone's past. History is history.

What does make sense is that schoolyard bullies become adult bullies in the workplace. Without a doubt, after 20 to 30 years of successfully intimidating and pushing around other people, by using humiliation as an interpersonal way of interacting, it will be very difficult, if not impossible, to stop an adult who's been reinforced for such conduct since grade school. Those people have no trouble looking you in the eye and calling you a loser, because their actions have been regularly reinforced.

In our society, we do a good job of drumming in the message of aggression. War metaphors abound. Don't just win; obliterate the competition. But don't buy into that. The ones who absorbed those messages like sponges are now working for you!

The problem is socialization, not only of the individual within families but by institutions such as the schools. So although it lends itself to good explanations for why bullies bully, there's actually nothing you can do about any of those factors. You cannot resocialize individuals. Great to know for Monday-morning sociologists, but the explanation is essentially useless.

The Bully's Personality

So, let's turn to what you probably believe to be the primary cause of bullying: personality of the bully.

Hateful, despicable, aggressive people are clearly antisocial. Bullies are narcissistic and egocentric. Most successful bullies harm other people and organizations. However, none of that means that they necessarily are people with certifiable personality disorders. People with antisocial personality disorders began their aggression in adolescence. This includes behaviors such as pulling wings off of bugs or throwing cats into microwaves just for curiosity's sake. There is new research that focuses on adolescents with conduct disorders, the ones on the way to becoming lifelong lawbreakers, that revealed activation of pleasure zones in their brains when they witness a person suffering pain.

That person in the cubicle next to you may not want to cooperate as much as you would like, but that doesn't mean he or she has an antisocial personality disorder. Let's reserve that label for the seriously unbalanced and the meanest among us.

To be narcissistic is to have an inflated sense of self. Narcissists like to hang around one another and refuse to interact with people who they think are beneath them. They feel a bonding, a kinship, with others who also feel naturally superior. But just because your world revolves around you doesn't mean you have a narcissistic personality disorder.

Narcissism is probably a dominant value in contemporary American culture. Otherwise good people may act selfishly and engage in constant self-promotion and self-marketing because they believe that's the only way to survive, let alone succeed. Luckily, everyone who is full of himself or herself does not have a personality disorder.

The most extreme personality explanation for bullying is that the bully is a psychopath. Dr. Robert Hare, North America's preeminent expert on psychopathy, has developed a checklist of traits and attributes of psychopaths. His list includes the need for constant stimulation without which there is a proneness to boredom. However, that means that it is unlikely that your bully is a psychopath, because psychopaths would not tolerate a 9-to-5 job. There is no clock-punching for them. Hare estimates that 1 in 100 executives is psychopathic, and he laments, as do we, that society is growing more psychopathic all the time.

Hare's work formed the basis for the 2004 documentary *The Corporation*.[25] In that film, the traits and attributes from his checklist described various corporate decisions that hurt people, damaged the environment, and showed a recklessness that individual psychopaths display. It's worth viewing.

Another, and our preferred, alternative to narcissism is Machiavellianism. Machiavellians are prototypical Americans. They are ambitious. They use other people to help them accomplish their goals. They are willing to exploit other people, not necessarily because they consider others as inferior, but simply because they are objects that can help them get ahead.

The psychologist Richard Christie, who developed Machiavellianism as a measurable personality trait, was careful to distinguish it from amorality. It's not about lacking morals; it's simply about ambition driving actions against others to get a personal win. Stanford professor Rod Kramer, in a 2006 *Harvard Business Review* article,[26] implored us all to give more credit to those who possess superior "political intelligence." He argued that visionary, great leaders are essentially beneficent exploiters of others in order to accomplish great goals. Yes, some are narcissistic, but their political skills are why they rose to the top and deserve to have others beneath them play a role in their grand design (and, we are supposed to be glad to have been part of the great man's purpose).

But frankly, aren't we sick of politicizing everything? In the United States, we live in a constant election cycle, either two or four years long. It's all about winning the office, never about doing the performance when in office. All process, never outcomes. All posturing, never results. So, we think "political intelligence" is vastly overrated. Politics is heartless, polarizing, and ruthless and passes for entertainment over which the media obsess. Imagine a world where politics plays a smaller role (of course, as we argue, this is the naive perspective of a target who wants to ignore the politics of the workplace conspiring against him or her).

Back to Machiavellianism. In its relatively benign form, a modicum of Machiavellianism seems required to accomplish most things. The simplest example is when it is invoked to get a job. One needs to appear sufficiently ambitious and driven. But when carried to a negative extreme, the needs of one person get trampled by an intimidator, making life a zero-sum game. Exploiters win only when others are obliterated.

The Target's Personality

Before we leave this discussion of personality, let's talk a bit about the personalities of people selected by bullies for torment. We call them targets, not victims. Three primary target traits have emerged from our nearly 15 years of intimate observation of thousands of bullied individuals.

First, targets tend to abhor confrontation and remain cooperative even when the game switches to fierce competition. When the rules stipulate that in order to survive you have to be competitive, sometimes strictly competitive as in a zero-sum game, or that you have to be simply Machiavellian in order to survive, targets choose to cooperate, enduring great personal sacrifice. They do not respond to aggression with aggression. This inability to confront the bully at the first chance is a lost opportunity that rarely presents itself again. One needs to capitalize on the immediacy of that first attempt when the bully is testing the waters. So, to turn one's back to walk away to fight another day proves very costly for targets.

Second, targets tend to be open and guileless. They are more open about their history and give insight into their susceptibility. We call this high self-disclosure. They see themselves as honest, forthright, and candid, with nothing to hide. The exploiters see them as easy prey. By contrast, aggressive and intimidating people tend to keep private matters private. They play things "close to the vest," allowing others to fill the often painfully long void with revelations that they can later use against targets. This is how they identify the psychological-emotional buttons to push later, ensuring that the target loses control of situations when in the bully's presence. Thus, the target gets punished for being open and honest.

Finally, the personality of targets is defiantly optimistic. They believe in a benevolent world. To them, the world is just and fair. Payoffs, rewards, and outcomes are commensurate with input, effort, and skill. Of course, it's not a fair world, and that presents the problem for targets. The traumatologist Ronnie Janoff-Bulman, in her book *Shattered Assumptions,*[27] summarized her research and identified the belief in a benevolent world. This belief is a deeply rooted sense of fairness and justice. One example of this thinking is, "If I treat the world in a just and fair way, fairness will be reciprocated." According to Janoff-Bulman, people holding this belief have the strongest likelihood of being traumatized when the expectation is violated. That belief was the difference between people who suffered posttraumatic stress disorder (PTSD) after exposure to potentially trauma-inducing events and people who did not develop PTSD. It seems to stem from a naivete and innocence shared by victims of abuse in families and at work.

Personality does not explain everything! Naturally, the problem is that traits and characteristics, like we just discussed, are relatively permanent for bullies and targets alike. There is no change possible. As an employer, you are powerless to change them.

To brand people with a personality disorder is to demonize them as unfixable. Mental health clinicians do not affix the label lightly. It can ruin a person's career or personal life. So, the problem when trying to stop workplace bullying is that if you get derailed down the personality track, you will pursue solutions that will get you absolutely nowhere. Here's our warning. Personality-obsessed solutions, such as anger management or dealing better with conflict by attitudinal change or anything that suggests changing an individual's personality, are doomed to fail.

So why do bullies bully? The simplest answer is because they can. And we, as organizational leaders, enable it. We set the stage. After all, we are the ones determining the number of positions there will be and setting the qualifications for people in those jobs, recruiting and selecting the people, assigning the workload, setting and measuring expectations, tracking the metrics, and so on. That entire list comprises a large part of the work environment. When you refer to the workplace climate or culture, you are referring to the work environment. And as leader, you are a major part of it.

The Power of Place over People

Instead of personality, let's explore how the work environment predicts performance and its deviant manifestation, bullying. The term *environment* has been used for years by managers in multinational firms accustomed to dealing with their Euro partners. It is a term used extensively by occupational health psychologists, epidemiologists, and management scientists when referring to workplace variables. If you feel more comfortable with *culture* or *climate*, simply make the mental substitution.

The work environment is a stronger and better predictor of how workers perform than personalities alone. The distinction between personality as a performance predictor and the work environment as a predictor is central to all of our work and the advice we give you in this book.

The reality, as illustrated by social psychologists and social scientists for nearly 50 years, is that the environment can sway an individual's behavior quite easily. Think of the power of peer pressure and conformity and how often we emulate successful people. Those of us with any social savvy are constantly adjusting to situations, to go with the flow. That is, our behaviors are primarily determined by external factors. Sometimes we are aware of control from the outside; most times it is automatic and we comply without awareness.

The mechanism by which we explain why things happen is called causal attribution. It's not just theoretical mumbo jumbo. It turns out that we all attribute or assign responsibility for causing things to either internal or external factors. The choice of fixing responsibility on internal factors, such as a personality trait or motivation, makes individuals personally responsible for their fate. When external factors are seen as the primary cause, invoking an environmental or situational explanation, the person is off the hook. What happened depends more on the situation and mitigating circumstances. It is clear that at work, instructions, task demands, and other people in the workplace can determine, to a great degree, what a person does.

It is well documented in the scientific literature that all of us, when observing other people's behavior, tend to blame that person too much for mistakes made and overcredit that person for successes accomplished. The overreliance on internal factors, while simultaneously ignoring a host of external explanations or factors, is called the fundamental attribution error.

Whenever our society is described as celebrity driven or as a "cult of personality," it is committing the fundamental attribution error. We hold people responsible for their actions, often without having supportive evidence and without bothering to discover evidence about other factors that could better explain events. That same error is at the heart of every failed internal organizational investigation of wrongdoing. Investigators blind to work environment factors will never conclude that the organization is at fault. Blame will always be on the accused individual.

7

Social Influence

How Others Define Our World for Us

Witnesses and Bystanders
Who Enable Bullying

We think it's worthwhile for you to understand how social factors can make people do things that they are not aware that they're doing. A real-world event that launched a lot of scientific inquiry happened in 1964 in Queens, New York. Kitty Genovese was a waitress returning home after a late-night shift. Mugged between the parking lot and the front stoop of her apartment building, she screamed in horror as she was stabbed repeatedly. The reason this mugging became so famous is because no one bothered to report the attack. Across the street from her apartment building was an equally tall apartment building facing hers. In response to her initial screams, dwellers in the building awoke, switched on their lights, and went to their windows to see what was wrong. We know from subsequent reports that there were 38 neighbors—38 witnesses—to the Genovese assault. Of course, the story became famous because not one of the 38 actually bothered to telephone the police. No one did that simple act that carried no risk. The wounded Ms. Genovese then stumbled to her building's entrance. By then the lights were off and all 38 left their windows and had retired. The mugger returned and completed the killing. Her final screams did result in one telephone call to the police, but it was too late to save her.

The *New York Times* reporter, later editor Abe Rosenthal, in his book *Thirty-Eight Witnesses* (republished in 1999), characterized New Yorkers as apathetic, unfeeling, and completely lacking in compassion given their failure to intervene to help Genovese. That negative stereotype lasted for generations until

September 11, 2001, and suddenly the altruism of New York first responders to the emergency became legend.

Two social psychologists, Bibb Latane and John Darley, made their research careers by recreating the circumstances for the Genovese murder witnesses. Their conclusion was that the people were not bad. Rather, each person was aware that there were other witnesses, and each thought someone else would call the police. The researchers called it "diffusion of responsibility." The larger the witnessing group, the lower the probability that any single individual will intervene became the maxim. The field of study was called bystander intervention, actually nonintervention. Later, this will become crucial in formulating ways to get coworkers to respond when they witness bullying incidents.

The bystander effect is one example of a larger set of illustrations called social influence. The presence of others whose actions are unknown diminishes the chance of intervening in an emergency. Other social influence studies demonstrate how susceptible we are to the definition of reality by others. Just hanging around a waiting room with a person who is giddily happy, making paper balls and shooting baskets, makes another person happier—and more likely to engage in that type of behavior. Being in a room that fills with smoke while others sit by doing absolutely nothing and not acknowledging the smoke leads people to simply sit through the smoke and not call for help.

Some of the strongest examples of social influence are modeling. We observe what others are doing, and if they have status in our minds (such as parents or bosses), we will most likely copy what they do when we see their behavior positively reinforced. It's easy to see how rewarded aggressive behavior gets copied. It works, so others are willing to do it. The message here is not to underestimate the power that others have over presumably objective circumstances.

Role-Dictated Behavior

Related to social influence is a remarkable 1974 study from Stanford University—the prison experiment.[28] Phil Zimbardo was the lead psychologist in establishing a mock prison in the basement of the university psychology building during summer school. Students were recruited to participate in a two-week study of prison life. Each was tested to rule out any psychological abnormalities. The students, all "normal" males, were randomly—remember, randomly—assigned to be either prisoner or guard. Prisoners were stripped of their dignity by being made to wear short, flimsy hospital gowns with no underwear. They were instructed to refer to each other by an assigned number and to follow commands given by guards. Guards were given uniforms and told to work an eight-hour shift. They received no instructions. They were left to fill time as they saw fit.

To the surprise of the professor and the overseeing graduate students, the experiment was shut down after only five days. The first anxiety breakdown happened on day three. That prisoner wanted to quit but was goaded into staying by five fellow prisoners. One guard grew increasingly mean and violent. Most guards made prisoners do push-ups and ask for simple rights, such as to eat or use the bathroom. The takeaway lesson from this landmark study was that normal people could fall quickly into adopting roles as if they were in a play, and despite the artificiality of circumstances, the individuals acted out roles as they thought they were expected to do. It seems roles come with unwritten scripts. The prison script was totally improvised and acted out wholeheartedly by the participating students and faculty.

We think it's obvious how managerial and supervisory expectations without the benefit of specific training can lead to disastrous results. The guards grew aggressive in the study when given complete freedom to act as they wished and relied on stereotypes about prison guards, probably based on bad movies or television shows. They were conforming to unstated expectations.

Similarly, many managers think that aggression is what's expected of them. Throw into the mix the observation by newer, younger supervisors of aggressive senior managers getting rewarded and you have nearly guaranteed the style of management you will see. To be rewarded, the person does not have to be promoted or receive a paid bonus. It is sufficient not to be stopped. To bully with impunity is itself rewarding and sure to sustain the misconduct.

There is typically a glaring juxtaposition between official pronouncements stating that disrespect is wrong (in those ubiquitous statements of mission, vision, and values) and in-the-trenches aggression between individuals. Observed, successful, and expected conduct is a better predictor of how managers manage. If aggression is expected, it happens reliably. Words pale compared with actions and observed consequences.

One other reason for bullying makes us reluctant to even mention it: people bully others because they are simply following orders. They are told when they are first assigned to a new unit to "clean up" the mess down there. In other words, the manager has some leftover grudges that he or she wants settled. Bullying is the way to finish the work that the original manager started. We say we're reluctant to mention it because if you genuinely want bullying to stop (after all, you did buy this book), you're probably not the type of manager to order it done on your behalf. However, just as managers bully because they think that that's what they should be doing, there are many managers who bully simply because they are doing what they are instructed to do.

Now to return to our explanation of why bullying happens, which is really the question we should be asking. Let's combine the concepts of the explanatory power of both work environments and people who surround us into a model that allows us to re-engineer what needs to be changed in order to stop the bullying.

8

A Model of Preventable Causes of Bullying

Our model has three components: the cutthroat work environment, the people, and the employer's response. The first and third aspects are completely in the employer's control: control the work environment to stop bullying. The first aspect is that the workplace environment, or climate, is cutthroat. Somehow, winner-take-all has become a zero-sum, strictly competitive way of dealing with others in the workplace. It's obvious in a sales organization how employees can quickly develop cutthroat strategies. Scrambling for limited funds, office space (as so comically depicted in the film *Office Space*), or the privilege of just holding on to a job can create a cutthroat culture.

Competition can arise simply when there is scarcity, real or imagined. In other words, when there's not enough funding to go around, not enough status to be granted, or not enough desirable tasks to assign, scarcity exists. There can also be the employee perception of scarcity even when it doesn't exist. That perception is all it takes to get workers scrambling for goodies. It's very easy to pit worker against worker in tough, lean times.

From our consulting practice, we've found some of the highest bullying rates in education. Why is this? Schools and universities are not sales organizations; they do not have sales contests. Funding scarcity is a reality in both K–12 and in higher education. Budgets are tight, and staffing cuts prevail. These institutions dedicated to teaching have inadvertently become fertile ground for abuse within their respective workforces.

Part 1: Cutthroat Culture

There can be no security where there is fear.
—Felix Frankfurter

Culture is set by chief executive officers (CEOs). The workplace tone, whether positive and empowering or cutthroat and destructive, is in leadership's hands. In the book *Winning*,[29] Jack Welch describes how to deliberately pit worker against worker to "allow the cream to rise to the top." But you have to be willing to designate 10 percent of the workforce unworthy and scheduled for termination. Relying on the fear of losing one's livelihood is Welch's motivational tool. If you are that type of leader, then bullying within the ranks is good. It destabilizes everyone. It keeps workers worried and guessing.

More likely, a cutthroat culture has developed without your awareness or deliberate intention. How could this happen? By default, organic development in our capitalistic society. It happens if you do not specifically declare to workers how you expect them to behave. Backstabbing, betrayal, and undermining authority are exactly the types of behaviors that will naturally emerge from a work group. Positive behaviors require clear expectations, constant attention, monitoring, and reinforcement. Negative emotions and negative conduct emerge when no attention is paid. Negativity dominates unless you, as leader, take deliberate steps to preclude it.

The notion of a Darwinian, survival-of-the-fittest mentality explains bullying very well. It converts the workplace into a jungle. The players in that jungle jockey for status as the "alpha" dominators and intimidators, regardless of gender. Fitness, it seems, is primarily based on strength or the followers' perceptions of that individual's strength. Leaders are effective based solely on their ability to control others. This is another explanation for those already in power to justify continued aggression. Countervailing evidence shows that our social networks and intragroup behaviors are not as simplistically Darwinian as the powerful want to believe they are. We will discuss this briefly in the next chapter.

Related to this is a laissez-faire style of management. Bad things happen outside of your control while you're not watching. You cannot delegate responsibility for vigilance over the interactions of workers in your units and divisions and still have a violence-free, bullying-free workplace. This means that if you want to stop bullying, you have to pay attention. It is an active art. You cannot manage on autopilot.

Part 2: People Mix

The second factor in our model is the necessary mix of people within the organization. Sprinkle some narcissists and exploiters within a pool of people who believe it is a fair and benevolent world and the recipe is complete. Remember when we said that health care was a field plagued by bullying? This is because there are so many people that entered the industry with nothing more than a desire to heal and to help people. A vast number of these individuals have an all-too-realistic, prosocial orientation. These helpers tend to focus on patients and families. The exploiters, the bullies, focus on internal politics to bring others down. That's why bullying is so rampant in health care.

Of course, this is true in any profession where good-hearted people populate the workforce. Some of the saddest and most hypocritical cases we've ever heard come from workers in domestic violence shelters. Their only task is to help the abused. However, they are harassed by abusive managers and coworkers rather than being left alone to do the work they cherish. Our experience with them taught us long ago that no type of work-place is immune from an infestation of bullies.

It should come as no surprise that the corporate world is also full of examples of blustering bullies. We encountered an information technology (IT) manager whose rages and draconian rules had driven 17 of his 24 workers to file discrimination complaints. Unfortunately for the workers, nearly everything he did was legal. The filings were the workers' dramatic plea for help that never came. We left the weeklong visit with the company reasonably certain that the basis of the manager's resentment was grounded in the fact that he possessed absolutely no skill with computers, hardware, software, the end-user experience, or information systems. The IT workers cared little about office politics, preferring to stick to technical aspects of their craft. It was the perfect pairing between exploiter and the apolitical exploited folks.

When looking at this second component of our model, the people mix factor, we know that employers do not adequately screen job applicants for a destructive aggressive streak. If they did, there wouldn't be so many bullies. However, recall that Machiavellians simply appear ambitious. They give great interviews. And most hyperaggressive people are quite bright. All this adds up to the bullies getting in.

The targets are hired typically because they possess the requisite skills that the organization wants. And they have a great customer service orientation because they are eager to please others. The profile of targets (based on our 2003 study) is that they refuse to be subservient, are technically more skilled than their bully, are well liked, are ethical and honest, and abhor workplace politics.

What employers really should be doing during the recruitment and hiring process is screening for bullies to keep them out. This, however, is not always the popular opinion. A counselor in Britain developed an instrument to detect potential *targets* of bullying with the notion that organizations should not hire people prone to suffer if and when they are abused. To us, this seems rather backward. Given the talent that targets bring to organizations, this seems foolish. To screen out the abusers and to protect the abused seems a more humane and wise plan.

Employers can and should deliberately shape the workplace culture to prevent cutthroat behavior from ever developing. This is the first component in our model. There is little to be done about the mix of aggressors and altruists in the employee pool, the second component. You live with the staff on hand. The hiring process is past. Our Blueprint system to stop bullying (explained later) works with the intact workforce. However, employers are instrumental in the establishment and maintenance of bullying, which is directly tied to how they respond to bullying when it is reported. This is the third component. In other words, employers have tremendous leverage over the first and third components of our model. They should take advantage of the amount of control they enjoy.

Part 3: The Employer Response

The third part of our model is the employer response to bullying incidents when they become known. After bullying incidents are actually reported to people in authority, most American employers react in ways very different from how targets expect them to respond.

In 2008 we conducted an online survey. We asked bullied targets what their employers did when they reported the bullying. Respondents said the employer did nothing (53 percent) or conducted a biased or inadequate investigation (40 percent). Employers got credit for conducting a fair investigation in only 7 percent of the cases. Not acting—doing nothing—is not a neutral act. When someone asks for relief from stress-inducing circumstances, to respond by doing nothing is to reject the legitimacy of the request. Couple that request with an emotional desperateness where the person's identity is under attack and a "do nothing" reaction conveys a sense of being undeserved. It's all very dehumanizing and belittling.

As discussed earlier, if the conduct is rewarded explicitly or implicitly, by virtue of trying to ignore it, it will be reinforced and will continue. This is simply the rule of positive reinforcement and operant conditioning theory determining real-world consequences. From the bully's perspective, bullying carries very little risk. In a WBI 2009 online survey, we asked targets (bullies do not make themselves available for research for countless reasons!) what happened to their bullies after the misconduct was reported. Absolutely nothing happened to 54 percent of the bullies, 28 percent were rewarded, 14 percent were investigated, and only 4 percent were punished or terminated. No consequences equals impunity. That outcome grants the blank check to continue unabated. Rewards typically involved promotions in rank. Yes, as a result of being identified as a bully (more likely called harassers), individuals rose up the organization chart!

The message to targeted workers and their allied witnesses and coworkers is clear: Aggression is rewarded. If you want to drive out negative behavior, the consequences have to change. There has to be a reengineering of the link between action and consequence. It's not rocket science. However, it takes a great deal of willpower and executive self-confidence to accomplish the necessary reengineering. That is what our Blueprint system entails.

You have no control over the personality of individuals. What you do have control over is this: several work environment factors that you may not have considered to be important before. We hope we've shown how strongly these factors can account for bullying. To stop the bullying, read on and learn how to specifically make those changes that are in your control.

9

Mobilize Your Organization

Leaders' Preparations

We begin the preparation at the highest level, in the C-suite. There is much to be done. The essential first element is recognizing the commitment of the pro-bullying forces ready to resist your campaign. Then, it's time for introspection. Leadership preparation finishes with specific tasks that lead you to an awareness of psychosocial factors that you control. With the factors well controlled, you deliberately create a healthy, bullying-free workplace.

It's a War

Bullies have declared war. They don't care about your mission, your responsibility to ensure fiduciary soundness, or your commitment to the health and well-being of the majority of employees. Bullying prevents work from getting done. It undermines your mission. It satisfies only the perpetrator's personal agenda, and it does so at the expense of people, their productivity, and their passion. It is the antithesis of work. And the only simple way to distinguish "tough" management from bullying is to ask, "What has this (action) got to do with work?"

Ideally, we could approach the task as pacifists. We could preach the gospel of kindness, altruism, and reciprocated cooperation among all employees. In fact, that is exactly what Buddhism would lead us to do. (Although we doubt that the speed of transmitting the message of compassion would be quick enough to counter all of the aggression in our contemporary, hurried workplaces.)

But, because it is a war, we treat the campaign to stop workplace bullying as seriously as you would an external competitor. It requires preparation of various internal groups, the troops required for the battle ahead in order to win. As an aside, we are ambivalent about using any war metaphor to ensure respect and dignity for employees, however counterintuitive it may seem.

Aggression and its rewards are communicated throughout the organization at lightning speed. The research findings from game theory unequivocally show that it is suicidal for a cooperator to continue to choose a cooperative response, a submissive response, when competitor-opponents repeatedly choose aggression. What stops the aggressor is aggression.

Every day on the shop floor, in the cubicles, and in the corner offices, you see examples of the tough, intimidating person granting respect to those who dared to stand up to him or her and not to be cowed. Bullies respond positively to aggression. It is their language, spoken on their terms, although the respect is granted grudgingly. Of course, this is the dilemma for cooperative, nonaggressive individuals targeted by bullies. They do not respond with aggression; they are victimized and not respected from the beginning.

So, gird your loins for the war ahead. If you do not have the stomach to stop the unacceptable conduct, you risk losing the confidence of all of the other employees who are rooting for you to stop the bullying. It's your choice: stay in denial and coddle the few or protect the vast majority.

Preparing Leaders, Preparing Yourself

For some researchers, bullying is a public health catastrophe. That being said, it might help for you to characterize the anti-bullying initiative as trying to address a disease. Bullying is a malignancy that invades your workplace. The problem metastasizes and threatens the functional integrity of your company, agency, or ministry. Like any undesirable cancer, it must be neutralized and eventually excised. Your organization's health cannot be restored if it is ignored.

We will strive to make this antibullying campaign toward a healthier workplace as impersonal as possible. No one (except bullies themselves) wants to launch a premeditated attack on another person. Our approach has the advantage of helping you purge destructive jerks, weasels, and snakes through means that remove the personality factor from the purging process. They will cease their destruction and join the workforce as a constrained human, or they will leave, mostly of their own volition. Their banishment is a secondary benefit you derive from faithfully implementing the steps we describe.

> *Leadership is based on inspiration, not domination; on cooperation, not intimidation.*
>
> —William Arthur Ward

Preparation begins at the top, with you. The board, C-suite team, and senior leadership must unequivocally want to eradicate bullying. If you are not ready, start this book over. Remind yourself why bullying must be dealt with. If you are ready, there are three Herculean tasks required to prepare the leadership team.

Leader Task 1: Recognize the Bullying around You

If division manager Bob is the one who keeps your company from earning the distinction as a "great place to work," then you have to face the fact that Bob is a problem. What got you to this point of scratching your head about the bullying is that Bob is your buddy. You have never seen Bob as a problem. He's become your friend both at work and socially.

Bob has been ingratiating himself to you for so many years that you associate feeling good with his presence. That's been his sole job, pleasing you. He has always been agreeable. He has never dissented. He has lavished you with undeserved praise for ideas that were sometimes yours, sometimes the team's, sometimes good, and sometimes not so brilliant. And when you looked around for people to promote, to give high-profile desirable projects, Bob always came to mind. In a way, you've been conned.

To the team, Bob has been a problem for years. His profits are overestimated. His productivity reflects more stealing credit from others than actual accomplishments. His apparent loyalty is actually more fickle than you imagined. He has a backup plan to leave the company on a whim. Bob's staffers hate him and transfer out at the first possible chance. However, the only portrayal of Bob to which you've been privy has come from Bob himself. He is the master of managing your impression of him.

Therefore, the first step in your personal preparation for stopping workplace bullying is for you, the leader, to take a step back and assess the situation. Separate your defensiveness about the incompetent, but politically connected, "Bobs" in your organization from the evidence about them. The only mistake you have made is to trust a "friend." Early in the process of converting your organization from a bullying-prone to bullying-free environment, you will have to request, collate, and then abide by empirical evidence about the performance of the Bobs. Find out what the majority of people working under the Bobs have to say about their work world. Friendships with managers who have a documentable history of destroying coworkers and subordinates threaten to undermine your ability to lead. You cannot be credible with the majority of employees unless and until you make the separation.

You need to not only be perceived as technically competent and able to rally the workforce to accomplish defined goals (a simple definition of leadership) but also be benevolent toward workers. In a major theoretical paper on leadership, Mark Van Vugt, Robert Hogan, and Robert Kaiser applied evolutionary theory to the concepts of leaders and followers. Remember when we discussed the fact that many bosses and managers justified their aggression based on treating the workplace as a Darwinian jungle? This paper challenges the conventional wisdom.

Van Vugt et al., the authors of the seminal 2008 article in the *American Psychologist*,[30] posited that the biological remnant of the earliest human experiences in groups (when we lived in genetically related tribes that evolved into larger groups more than 2.5 million years ago) depended primarily on demonstrated competence by leaders. For those millions of years, groups were primarily democratic, thanks to subordinates who rejected dominating leaders. Leaders had to share resources or face challenges to their status through rebellion. In other words, most of our inherited experience with leadership and followership shaped benevolent, as well as competent, leaders.

According to those same researchers, our brain's biological experience with unilateral leaders who act without concern for the needs of the group dates back to only 13,000 years ago, at the end of the last Ice Age. Therefore, inherent in human followers is a more permanently established expectation that leaders need to show fairness, goodness, and a willingness to share.

We heard Tom Chappelle, the founder of Tom's of Maine (a company specializing in all-natural personal products), speak, and he described his failed search for meaningful values in business schools. He found divinity school to be the only place where humane treatment of others was a central aspect of the teachings. Business schools too often produce "pillars of society" known best for the accumulation of personal wealth through fraudulent transactions, or at least unethical ones, if barely legal.

How equitable is the contemporary American organization where the average CEO earns 263 times the average salary of a nonsupervisory worker?[31] So much for sharing resources!

Leader Task 2: Trust Reports from the Trenches

Empathic leaders, once referred to as social-emotional leaders, function and make decisions as if they remember what it was like to be in the lower ranks. They intuitively know how much workers want to be believed and how much they want to contribute to make the workplace better. Good leaders trust employees. Good employees can be counted on for internal intelligence and fact gathering. They are compensated for their work and double their worth when giving you information that consultants discover at a much higher cost. Executives who ignore in-the-trenches information from concerned employees jeopardize their organizations' success.

One of the most important ways you can show trust to employees is to believe reports of bullying when they bubble up to your level. Do not immediately discount them as frivolous or untruthful. It takes courage for targets to dare to tell higher-ups about bullying tactics in their units. They are providing much-needed intelligence for you. Do not shoot the messenger simply because you learn that Bob has a dark side. Just because he never showed that destructive side to you doesn't mean Bob is not cruel to subordinates. It makes sense. Bob has both sides. So do you; we all do. Contrast how you address shareholders in formal settings with how you communicate daily with peers and those who report to you. Depending on who is describing you, you, too, could be perceived as two completely different people. The same is true for bullies.

Although we want you to trust reports from the trenches, we also suggest that you not automatically accept the report of an employee. Test the veracity of the report. A true story can pass the following test.

Truth-Testing the Report

1. Gauge the impact on the person's health. If the person complains of an inordinate amount of stress from working with the accused bully, ask for evidence—absences ordered by a physician or therapist, a sudden change in the person's use of paid time off compared with a period before contact with the alleged bully, and symptoms that are embarrassing to share with you and unlikely to be fabricated. People lie about being stronger than they are. They do not boast about how devastated they are from repeated humiliation.

2. Search for corroboration. Have someone (not HR, but someone from your office) attempt to talk to coworkers to search for similar reports. Witness that, once your representative visits the scene of the bullying, everyone notices and watches fearfully the closed-door sessions. Your best bet is to call coworkers away, one at a time to another location. Note their uniform reluctance to talk, however, as evidence of a fear-plagued workplace where a bully's implied or explicit threats can account for the silence. If matters have escalated to a breaking point, they all may be willing to speak to finally get relief. In those rare circumstances, all will corroborate the report from the bullied target.

3. Search for the alleged perpetrator's pattern. Have HR provide you with a record of complaints, formal or informal, about the alleged bully over the course of his or her employment. Pattern and practice will typically emerge. Over the years, there have probably been multiple targets and targets

reporting multiple episodes. Perhaps other workers have tried to tell you about the alleged bully before but were kept away from you by your staff. Find out.

When authentic, empathic leaders learn how bullies damage organizations, they cannot afford to continue to ignore the problem. That's why you found this book.

To summarize the first two tasks for leaders: Do not deny that bullying happens in the organization you lead. Be open to reports that friends might be among the worst offenders. Demonstrate empathy for employees and believe the reports they bring to your attention. Commit to action and do not cover up the behavior or retaliate.

Leader Task 3: If You Are the Problem, Admit It and Stop

It's one thing if Bob is the problem person. The spread of the problem depends on the rank of the bully and how that person can control the workplace culture for many employees. On the other hand, if you are a senior executive, your negative influence over the organization is greater than anyone else's. The span of despair you could create is unrivaled. So, be careful. We tell people to extricate themselves from bullying workplaces in which the bully is the CEO.

So, how do you know if you are the problem? Here are some warning signs. Check to see how many apply.

Warning Signs That You Are the Bully

- Your job is solely to be the visionary leader, focused only on the marketplace and competitors. Managing and internal operational details are done by others.

- In meetings, your positions are rarely, if ever, challenged as inappropriate or wrong.
- You are always surprised that colleagues and lower-level managers do not have the same high performance standards you have.
- You understand the merits of collaborative decision making, but in the final analysis, and for expediency, the decision is yours.
- Department managers you personally appointed/promoted experience the highest rates of turnover or transfer requests compared with other managers.
- You are straightforward and honest when evaluating others. Yet, others often misunderstand or do not appreciate your "style."
- If a decision you've made proves to be a critical failure, it was based on incomplete or inaccurate information provided to you.
- It takes a special type of person to succeed in roles supporting you. Your staff changes often.
- When you are told that one or more groups of employees are experiencing high levels of "stress," you feel it is the responsibility of those employees to better manage their feelings and perceptions.
- Fear motivates staff. It prevents complacency and sharpens the mind. It produces optimal performance.
- People in general are followers. Leaders must demonstrate resolute certainty and unwavering principles.
- You prize loyalty within the leadership team above all other values. A cohesive team can guide an organization through turbulent markets and economic crises.

Use the self-assessment to be aware of your role and its potential impact on the subsequent antibullying initiative.

Leader Task 4: Support the Antibullying Campaign

You can support the antibullying effort in your organization by funding the startup and not interfering with the subsequent procedures to comply with a new policy. When our Blueprint system is implemented fully, you (as well as everyone else) will be held accountable for violations, that is, for bullying. Hundreds or thousands in your organization are hoping to make their workplace free from bullying. Please make that happen.

In meetings, where so much bullying is manifested, designate on a rotating basis a formal dissenter. That person, regardless of his or her personal opinion, has to shoot holes into decisions made by the group. Make, and abide by, the rule that ideas are disembodied things, not attached to their inventors. Foster true innovation by enabling free thinking. Critical thought that requires dissent rather than robotic agreement produces better decisions. Let go of the control (as impossible as this sounds). For fun, be sure to take your turn as designated dissenter. You will find yourself seeing the downside of some of your best ideas. It's a good cognitive stretch exercise.

Bullies use meetings to insult and dehumanize team members they don't like. If you get a warning that you have just leveled someone in a very hurtful way, make an adjustment. You may have thought that you were merely correcting that person. From the recipient's point of view, it was a devastating blow to his or her integrity. How would you react if someone had the temerity to call you and your ability to think hopeless and embarrassing? The lesson here is to devise a way to stop and think. The team with a long history with you is not going to voluntarily confront you about your unacceptable conduct if they have not done so already. You will have to listen to yourself and pause before delivering your message. Does your tone suggest aggression? How is your body language? Anticipate how you would feel if you were treated that way.

Support the antibullying program. The consequences of bullying are expensive, and you have the responsibility to maintain the organization's fiduciary soundness. Furthermore, by being an industry leader, you will have bragging rights for creating an abuse-free workplace for your employees. Let your visionary self embrace credit for doing good for so many.

Leader Task 5: Embrace the Value of Employee Health—Physical and Psychological

In the past, you might have delegated employee health and safety to a single person or "safety" department. Without involvement of executives, a rift quickly develops between stated commitments to safe working conditions and actual practices. Groups of safety officers regularly invite Gary to speak at their conferences. He's learned that safety is not on any executive's list of priorities.

We're not asking you to edit the text of Material Safety Data Sheets (MSDS). Sometimes funding for workplace safety is denied in your name but without your awareness. Preventable physical injuries happen all the time when corners are cut to help achieve budget savings demanded by the C-suite.

The BP oil platform explosion in the summer of 2010 is an illustrative example. Workers identified safety deficiencies prior to the explosion, but they were ordered by managers to ignore the procedural and safety violations. Being cheap and/or lazy caused the horrific environmental disaster that affected millions of Americans and wildlife as well as resulted in the deaths of 11 employees. BP suffered a public relations disaster. The explosion was arguably preventable. How many lives and billions of dollars could have been saved?

We're not sure you're old enough to remember the television commercial that originated in 1971 for the Fram oil filter. The gist was that a $5 investment (the price back then!) could prevent a costly valve job worth thousands of dollars later. The catchy slogan was "pay me now or pay me later." The slogan conveys the same meaning as the axiom "an ounce of prevention is worth a pound of cure."

In the chemical industry, you have to be knowledgeable about risks from exposure to toxic chemicals. You understand the necessity of protective equipment. What might surprise you is that some of the worst bullying supervisors we've had reported to us actually deny targeted workers access to necessary safety equipment in those industries. One Texas utility company employee was allowed to suffer fatal brain cancer to appease the malicious tactics of a supervisor who hated him. His job was to replace old transformers containing the highly toxic PCB (polychlorinated biphenyls, which consist of more than 200 separate chemicals). His supervisor never allowed the victim to wear protective gear as specified in the safety regulations. When he died, the workers' compensation board decision supporting the supervisor was under appeal. That is, they deliberately endanger workers' lives as part of their game of domination. Bet you never heard about this going on.

If your company requires workers to engage in hard physical labor, you may know about lost productivity from back injuries, as reported by the risk manager or the company's workers' compensation insurer. If the work involves nearly constant use of keyboards and computer screens, you surely know about real risks from repetitive strain injuries (RSIs) and musculoskeletal strain from improper ergonomics. In other words, the risks of *physical* injuries are necessarily a part of task planning and load distribution simply to keep the workforce healthy and productive. Unfortunately, safety officers, who try to reduce *physical* injury rates, are trained neither to recognize nor to minimize *psychological* injuries.

Workplace toxicity raises risks of psychological injuries, too. The toxicity comes from the "psychosocial work environment." Most factors are invisible, unlike measurable carbon dioxide levels in the air or distance from the CRT screen. Just the same, they affect employee health. And in workplaces with minimal physical demands, psychosocial factors probably play the more significant role in explaining how employees come to suffer stress-related health problems.

Managing Psychosocial Factors in the Workplace

Examples of psychosocial factors include task characteristics and the social interaction among workers. These factors can create undesirable and unsafe work conditions.

Task Characteristics

- *Workload:* Demand on the worker can be overwhelming or insufficient to stimulate and interest the worker.
- *Task distribution:* Assigning tasks among workers can be proportional and evenly shared across staff or disproportional, a sort of dumping too much on one or two designated (targeted and disliked) workers.
- *Work pace:* The pace is too fast for anyone to keep up due to technology, automation, or the setting of impossible deadlines.
- *Work breaks:* Breaks are not scheduled at predictable times or breaks are too far apart, including breaks to use the restroom. (The worst cases of denial we encountered were

reports of older women working on an assembly line in a poultry processing plant who were never given breaks and had to wear undergarments for incontinence because they had to soil themselves during their work shift.)

- *Task variety:* Assignments can be monotonous, mind-numbing, or blatantly undesirable in nature or both, and only targeted workers are required to complete them.

- *Skill utilization:* As with workload, it's a problem when the person does not possess the requisite skills and does not receive training to learn them. It is also a problem if the task is not sufficiently challenging, cognitively or physically.

Social Interaction among Employees

- *Perceptions of procedural justice:* This is the subjective opinion a worker has about being treated fairly in a manner consistent with how others are being treated. For example, the worker may ask, "Why do I have to fill out paperwork when others simply make an oral request?"

- *Decision-making participation:* The worker is granted or denied autonomy over his or her work rate, task priorities, and quality of completed product or service. The highest autonomy is experienced by craftspeople who produce something from start to finish with complete control over the process.

- *Coworker interdependency:* Solo work tasks foster isolation from others and make it easy for capricious rules to be made that prohibit interaction.

- *Performance evaluation/appraisal:* Problems include ambiguous and vague evaluative aspects of the job that do not adequately capture the true nature of the work performed, the overreliance on subjective loyalty scales, or the failure by managers to conduct appraisals (ever or on an ongoing schedule).

- *Learning opportunities:* Lack of learning opportunities is problematic when workers perform tasks for which they have not been trained (learning has been denied) and will be held personally responsible if failure ensues.
- *Security and predictability:* The threat of impending termination or unremitting exposure to an intimidating coworker or boss can traumatize an individual.
- *Psychological safety:* Working in a constant state of anxiety as a result of threats, humiliation, and intimidation generates a health-harming work environment for the employee.
- *Respectful and dignified treatment:* The worker is not held in regard as an equal and is treated with contempt (by management or coworkers), as if a lesser human being.
- *Social interaction:* The worker is denied connectedness. Whether it is simply social, non–work-related chitchat or interaction to complete work tasks, social contact is an essential component of human existence. Its deprivation can lead to severe psychological distress. (The 20+ suicides at the Foxconn factory [where high-tech gadgets are manufactured for American companies] in China in 2010 were traced back to this aspect of the assembly line work by the Chinese workers. Despite working shoulder-to-shoulder for 12 to 14 hours per day, coworkers were forbidden to speak to one another.)

The psychosocial factors just described share two common themes: (1) the quality of management skill involved and (2) the thoroughness of a manager's knowledge about the products made or services delivered. Good managers deliberately shape the work environment rather than allowing it to develop in an uncontrolled manner. In addition, they minimize the harm (described in Chapter 1) that work conditions can cause. They deliberately ensure that they themselves do not harm the staff.

Psychosocial Factors and Stress and Trauma

The link between psychosocial factors and stress-related health problems is a direct one. Targeted individuals are under assault. These assaults are threatening and are sources of stress—that is, stressors. Assaults set off a physiological and biological sequence that results in stress. This is not an imaginary sequence. The good news is that you can stop bullying without ever having to admit complicity in its establishment or maintenance. Instead, claim credit for launching the initiative for solely proactive reasons—to be the early adopter, the industry leader, or the company that cares most about its most valuable assets, its people, or because "it's the right thing to do."

Examples of employers showing they care about the psychological health of employees do exist. There is awareness in some major companies of clinical depression and its impact on worker productivity. Work is also affected when depression is brought from home to work. Depression is known to interfere with sleep, which in turn leads to counterproductive or endangering fatigue. Depression leads to a drop in concentration and a decreased ability to perform complex cognitive tasks that preclude optimal performance. A depressed employee is the antithesis of an engaged employee. But whether depression is caused by events at home or events at work, it affects all aspects of work life.

Depression may also be at the core of "presenteeism." Presenteeism is a measure of lost productivity by workers present at work but otherwise distracted by personal issues. One large study ($n = 375,000$) claims that 61 percent of total lost productivity and medical costs can be traced to presenteeism.[32]

The Corporate Alliance to End Partner Violence (CAEPV, an employer membership organization) wisely describes employees who are victims of domestic violence as being at risk personally and posing a security risk to their employers. The abuser knows where to find the victim—at work. An abuser who is a crazed killer presents a homicidal risk to the employer as well. For three reasons, CAEPV member companies invest in protecting the domestic violence victim: (1) to prevent a massacre on site, (2) to minimize the violence so that the employee-victim can remain productive and free of injury at work, and (3) to help the employee-victim, who is traumatized and deserves support. It's a win-win for the victim and employer. CAEPV claims that its member companies account for more than 1 million U.S. workers. Remember, we view bullying as domestic violence only in the workplace.

Employers are familiar with psychological trauma, too. Banks were probably the first to offer mental health counseling to employees who experience robberies, are threatened at gunpoint, or witness murders. This postevent counseling is called critical incident stress debriefing (CISD), and companies typically contract with local mental health providers to provide this service. The rationale for counseling is that shocked workers have to be able to heal before returning to a normal productive routine. Having a CISD plan demonstrates sympathy for traumatized innocent victims and witnesses whose ability to emotionally cope has been overwhelmed. CISD also helps the employer with return-to-work plans. Employers do not blame employees when violent customers or the general public cause the trauma. Robberies, like natural disasters and car accidents, are assumed to be random. All can cause severe emotional disruption, which can lead to posttraumatic stress disorder (PTSD). No rational person would think that the bank teller or the distraught homeowner after a tornado had invited the emotional injury that followed the life-shattering event.

Given the baby steps taken by employers toward understanding how traumatizing events can affect an individual's psychological health, we suggest even more progress is required. For instance, employees with no history of depression (or those who are stable and healthy but have been medically managing their depression for years) who are subjected to unrelenting exposure to a bullying boss will develop anxiety as a normal response. It's the stressor-stress link, known as the external stimulus–internal response. The psychosocial stressor is the bully. If the bully and target are not separated so that the target is made to feel safe, anxiety may intensify to panic attacks. Then, if the target cannot get out of harm's way (according to our WBI 2003 online study, the average length of exposure to a bully is up to 22 months), depression may begin. For those with previously controlled depression, it flares up again and becomes unmanageable again. This is the equivalent of a recovering alcoholic relapsing, but not by his or her own choice. Depression is experienced by 39 percent of targets (again, based on our 2003 study). Remarkably, for 30 percent of women targets and 21 percent of men targets, the injury they sustain from bullying is PTSD! Imagine a war wound created at work by another person who intentionally meant to harm the target.

The primary difference between employer reactions to employees who are victims of domestic violence and require CISD support and targets traumatized by bullying is that only the latter group is not believed. In fact, they are blamed for their fate. All three groups may suffer PTSD, but only bullied targets receive no support. The assailant-perpetrator-stressor is on the payroll, acting as an agent of the employer. To admit that the person was injured implies responsibility for the series of incidents that caused the psychological harm. It's the American way to blame victims for their fate. The prevailing thought is that if you are diagnosed with PTSD, you must have been weak and unable to adjust to (the bully's) destabilizing, but legal, conduct. So if you are bullied, it is your fault for not coping well.

Do you see the hypocrisy, the double standard? The only difference that matters is whether or not the perpetrator or stressor is outside the employer's control. This is the attribution theory we talked about in the last section. When stressors are external to the employer, employers are sympathetic toward employees. When stressors are internal, employers (and their attorneys) fight hard to blame employees who suffered (involuntarily, we add) severe emotional injuries lest they be held accountable for work conditions completely under their control.

So, if you take the courageous steps to stop bullying, do it for the sake of your employees' health. Psychological injuries from bullying are preventable. Prevent them.

Good Managers and Leaders Should Control Psychosocial Factors

When managers are left to learn how to manage people on their own, they tend to rely on shoddy stereotypes of "bosses" from television or the movies. Managing others should be taught. Organizational behavior classes in business education programs sensitize students to fundamental psychological principles that help them in real-world situations. One of those principles is that positive reinforcement follows desirable and correct actions and is the only way to ensure long-lasting, self-perpetuating good performance by employees. Without learning about the studies with rats, pigeons, and people, the untrained manager might think that barking commands in a way to that instills fear is the best way to treat workers (as seen on television). They would rise up the ranks (rewarded by executives who never knew that positives pay off more than negatives) only to be surprised when subordinates abandon them and rebel when they need loyalty from underlings the most.

But training budgets are routinely the first sacrifice in hard times. Tough times or not, find a way to train your managers in interpersonal skills. Bad bosses treat subordinates as undeserving humans. We are able to abuse and mistreat people and animals only if we consider them less deserving of the respect and dignity we expect to receive from others. Ignore people skills at your peril.

The first defense of a bully is always that he or she never learned an alternative way to treat others. As the bully's boss, see that appropriate training is received as soon as possible. As a mentor, you will be held responsible for the misconduct carried out in your name.

Good managers minimize psychosocial risk factors by matching tasks to people well, taking care to fairly distribute work. They employ inclusive techniques in meetings and one-on-one sessions, create fair pay policies guaranteeing an appropriate amount of social contact (sometimes by designing interdependent tasks that force people to rely upon each other), and are present and available for workers.

Managers who really know their work are perceived as the best leaders and considered trustworthy by the workers they manage. Too many managers flit from company to company not knowing the specific work or industry but acting confident that they possess the necessary managerial wherewithal to be successful at any job. They are the professional managers envisioned by Peter Drucker in his 1954 manifesto, *The Practice of Management.* For instance, New York City mayor Michael Bloomberg (himself a financial guru who turned to politics) replaced the head of the NYC schools with a magazine publishing industry CEO. She, Cathie Black, oversees a school district with 1.1 million students and several thousand union employees despite having no experience with either education or unions. When hired, she begged for time to "learn the issues that affect K–12 education." This is the American recipe for employee resistance, resentment, and sabotage.

Our 2003 WBI online study revealed that the lack of technical knowledge about the work was the second most frequent reason given by targets for why they were targeted. Targets know their jobs. However, when supervisors of targets perform in roles with which they are unfamiliar, they can be anxious about their lack of skill. No one wants to nakedly reveal a personal incompetence. That anxiety makes them less safe to be around. Bullying bosses who don't know their stuff may lash out at employees for reasons related to their fear of failure because they don't know their job.

Managers lacking knowledge about the work itself pose a psychosocial risk to employees when they set an inhumane work pace, hoard decisions that require information that only the employees have, assign denigrating work that underutilizes employees' skills, and are unable to train others in task-relevant skills. In addition, these managers set impossible deadlines because they don't know how long quality work takes to complete, and they dump a disproportionate load of undesirable tasks on a few employees simply out of ignorance about how the products are made or services delivered.

One final note for executives: Making your workplaces bullying-free is your responsibility. It is not HR's job. Bullying is too serious to be left to those without the power to compel compliance with new standards of practice or new ways to behave interpersonally.

Preparing the Governing Board

Executives tend to lead their boards on operational matters. The governance role of boards necessarily focuses their attention on strategic matters, not operational ones. Implementing the anti-bullying program is operational and in the purview of the chief executive. If the board must give fiscal approval for the project to move forward, then members must understand the value of the program to the entire organization. It is also helpful to invite a board member to participate in the collaborative policy-writing process (Blueprint step 2) described in the next section.

10

Mobilize Your Organization

Managers' and Supervisors' Preparation

There is overwhelming evidence that the higher the level of self-esteem, the more likely one will be to treat others with respect, kindness, and generosity.

—Nathaniel Branden

Overcome the "Boss Problem"

A funny thing happens to many supervisors when they are first promoted. Far too many allow their heads to swell, forgetting their beginnings in nonsupervisory jobs. People simply do not start out at the top. It's very easy to forget that fact when your head is swirling with an inflated sense of self that naturally accompanies a promotion.

New managers brought in from the outside or newly minted MBAs have no historical roots in the company. They had no previous connection to the people with whom they work. They had no previous loyalties or bonds. Troubles and difficulties they cause can all be traced their stereotypical expectations about what it means to be a "boss." Television shows and movies exploit these for fun. But the inherent inequality between a boss and subordinate is not funny. If that relationship is not handled with care, it can easily be misused to subjugate another human being.

New supervisors would be loath to suggest they have a slave working for them. Despite this, with the way many subordinates are routinely treated in the American workplace, it is not an exaggeration to say that the relationship is only slightly better than that of master and slave. It is disgraceful when one human being, with no identifiable difference from another person other than a job title or position on an organization chart, can act with total disregard for that other person. "Management" should not connote the right to capriciously withhold positive regard for another person or to deny that person his or her inherent dignity.

Having no history in work units allows managers to begin with a clean slate, theoretically. We only wish it were so in practice. Too many departing managers are quick to share their

101

biases, rumors, and gossip about work team members. If any attention is paid to that drivel, the new manager already has a designated target to begin to bully. Some new managers, aiming to please their own managers, do the bullying as agents. This is especially cruel. Historically persecuted workers initially experience relief when the bullying manager leaves. Yea! . . . The joy is short lived.

Imagine the surprise and shock caused by the start-up of a bullying campaign by the new manager for no apparent reason. Why, who knows? This is an irrational process. The new manager who bullies based on historical rumor is dishonest to himself or herself because there is no discernible rationale for the actions.

Supervisors who are promoted from within the ranks are weighed down with emotional baggage of their personal history with the group. They know where all the skeletons are buried and who offended whom and when and which grudges are worth keeping. For many, donning the supervisor's hat allows them to get even for perceived injustices from the past. They can't wait to exercise the authority to play "petty tyrant." This lying in wait is commonly called "paying your dues."

We discovered a 1960s questionnaire that predicted employee subservience in organizations. One of the subscales of that now out-of-print instrument (called the WEPS: Work Environment Preferences Scale) was called self-subordination. Self-subordination reflects a willingness to comply fully with the stated wishes of superiors and to have decisions made by higher authorities. It described acts most people today would consider groveling, such as one's first real loyalty should be to a superior, people at higher levels are in the best position to make important decisions for people below them, and so on.

In real terms, this means keep your head low so as not to draw attention to yourself for any reason, good or bad. Believe in the goodness of management to do the right thing for workers. It seems accurately descriptive about boss-subordinate conduct in a bullying culture. Trust tends to go in only one direction—up the ladder, with ridicule and intimidation flowing downward from bad bullying bosses. Targets feel compelled to not complain when accosted by bullying bosses, not only for fear of retaliation but also because "taking it" is understood to be part of any job.

When supervisors were merely colleagues to coworkers, they certainly could cause misery to someone they hated. As bosses, they have the authority to threaten the withdrawal of that person's livelihood. The stakes are higher for the targeted former colleague, who is now at much greater risk.

In his 2010 book *Good Boss, Bad Boss*, Bob Sutton does discuss, at the insistence of his wife, he admits, examples of good behavior by managers. It is important work. It's just that it is not the focus of this book. We know it happens. Before bullying invaded our lives and dictated our professional work, we knew good folks working everywhere. When you specialize in bullying, as we have done for the past 14 years, there is an understandable immersion in the dark side of the world of work. We deal primarily with horrific situations. To their credit, the bold representatives of companies that bring us in to stop the bullying are the good people. They are all good bosses.

From the 2007 WBI U.S. Workplace Bullying Survey, we know that 35 percent of all targets of bullying are managers; this is summing together first-line supervisors, mid-level managers, and senior managers. On the other hand, 72 percent of all bullies outrank their targets by at least one level in the organization chart. Sadly, for managers, the stereotype about bullies being bosses is true. The proportion of bosses who are bullies is difficult to estimate.

If management could be made to stop bullying, there would be no need for policies, HR, or laws. It would all be handled informally. Our purpose in writing this book is to guide leaders through our Blueprint process precisely because informality doesn't work. Allow us to indulge in speculation about how managers could prevent and immediately eradicate bullying.

In this ideal, wished-for work world, managers would accomplish the three tasks discussed next.

Manager Step 1: Recognize Bullying

Bullying can be theatrical when done in front of an audience, in hallways, and in meetings. The bully is trying to control the emotional tone and can get somewhat histrionic. Tactics include yelling, swearing, screaming, threats, intimidating gestures, and verbal abuse. The perpetrator's goal is to freeze the target into submission with fear. Simultaneously, witnesses are expected to also quiver in fear that they might fall prey next and to do nothing to interrupt the show.

In our book *The Bully at Work*, we describe the performer as the screaming Mimi. Acts are overt, with motives transparent to even the most inexperienced observer. It would be a funnier show if it were not so harmful. Witnesses, as well as targets, risk being traumatized.

More detective skill is required to discern bullying that happens behind closed doors. Constant critic-type bullies choose private settings to undermine their targets' confidence in their competence. Being out of sight gives the bully a shot at plausible deniability if what transpires ever becomes known through a complaint or lawsuit. The bully can simply deny what was done. And HR uncritically will accept the denial as the credible "other side" of the story. Employment attorneys also defend the bully's actions based on managerial prerogative. What typically happens is that a supervisor new to management decides to attack a veteran accomplished employee. The choice of weapon is a fabricated performance evaluation shockingly opposite to the prior years of superlative praise heaped on the worker. By keeping the humiliation behind a closed door, the target's shame is magnified.

Two-headed snake–type bullies aim to control their targets by damaging reputations. Rumors are the tools bosses and co-workers use to circulate false facts throughout the organization. When the target becomes aware and attempts to counter the lies, it sounds like rationalization, excuse making. The first portrayal of the target's abilities or personality attributes, regardless of mendacity, is the one that sticks. Sometimes the defamatory depiction is between a supervisor from whom the target is transferring to the new supervisor. The lies prejudice the new supervisor. The target is already in a one-down position the first day on the new job when, in fact, he or she expected freedom from abuse for the first time in a long time.

Gatekeeper-type bullies are the prototypical "control freaks." When they are managers, they micro-manage. They care less about actual performance than taking sadistic delight in how much control they can exert over a target's working conditions. One of their favorite tactics is to withhold resources that their direct reports require to succeed in their jobs. They deny training when assigning people to new tasks. They physically and psychologically separate (by commanding coworkers to ostracize) workers to deny them routine social contact. They also exploit workers at times of great personal vulnerability. They attack the first day back from prolonged sick leave to recover from a stress-related heart attack. And the most sadistic episode ever reported to us was a supervisor who forbade coworkers from calling 9-1-1 to assist their friend who had collapsed with a heart attack right before their eyes. (The man survived but only because one person defied the order. The subsequent lawsuit was settled for seven figures so the employee never had to work again. The supervisor suffered no known consequences.)

Manager Step 2: Intervene Whenever Possible

Courage is fire, and bullying is smoke.
—Benjamin Disraeli

Most people think intervention requires you to jump between the two parties just before the bully is about to take a swing. Not necessarily true. To do that you would have to be a witness to the bullying incident right there on the spot. What are the chances? Rather than taking immediate action, it is more likely that you will hear about the incident after it happened. Then, there is time to plan your delayed, post hoc intervention.

After the antibullying Blueprint program has been fully engaged, interventions by managers may be mandated or, at least, strongly suggested. It may become a new managerial responsibility. But prior to the formalization, it makes sense to attempt to intervene on behalf of the targeted employee.

Delayed interventions can be very effective because so few people have the courage to do them. Bullies are shocked that someone dare confront them, and they really admire and respect those aggressive enough to do so.

If the target works in your unit, intervention is part of your job right now. Don't try to dodge the problem with the excuse to employees to "work it out between yourselves." Get to work and make the bullying stop.

Suggestions for Interventions

- Get the target to safety and give extra paid time off (while not depleting the employee's paid time off banked days).
- Require the target to provide a timeline of details of all incidents to help determine cause and effect.

- Ask the target how the alleged misconduct has affected work production, health, reputation, and so forth, and require evidence of adverse consequences or damages.
- Synopsize the complaint for the bully (or all perpetrators, if more than one) and share the accusation.
- Solicit the bully's reaction and rationale for the conduct.
- Know the most frequent explanations bullies give: (1) I was doing what I thought I was expected to do, (2) This is nothing more than a misunderstanding by the target of my intentions, or (3) I'm being misperceived; I'm the victim here. (Plan how to reverse the bullying if one or more are true.)
- Attempt to interview the other employees to determine whether they ever witnessed anything. Expect very little cooperation and lots of fear.
- Consult with HR to determine what existing policies (such as those related to violence, perhaps, which routinely include the prohibition of verbal abuse) or codes of conduct might govern the types of misconduct alleged.
- Do not attempt to put the bully and target across the table from each other to find common ground (mediation) unless the bullying has caused no severe consequences for the target.
- Innovative remedies may include a restatement of your expectations about how coworkers must interact and a clarification by the bully to the target about his or her intentions, followed by an apology, unpaid leave for the bully, and counseling for the target by a mental health professional.
- Share the remedies with the target and bully and share your decision about what actually occurred with any workers who assisted in your inquiry (shutting out individuals who helped at great risk because of "confidentiality" undermines your credibility).

- Add to a future team meeting's agenda your explicit expectations about how people are to treat one another and include yourself as part of the team to be held accountable; then discuss by soliciting reactions from everyone, paying special attention to the bully's contribution to the discussion.

Those are our suggestions for how to address bullying within your team, relying on delayed interventions. But what if you witness a target being bullied in another work team? We advise you to take mental or actual notes about the incident and sit down with that team's manager, your peer. Report what you saw and heard. If that manager is not sure what to do or prefers to compel the bully and target to solve the problems themselves, share with your peer your strategy as outlined previously. You may have to mentor.

If you observed a peer manager acting like a bully in front of others, you should confront the peer in private. Provide that supervisor with the historical and objective facts about the targeted employee's contributions to the organization. Suggest that building a case to terminate that specific worker (which the bully most likely wants to do) serves no organizational need and would be an injustice.

Finally, there will be opportunities to intervene when you are the manager of a supervisor that an employee has accused of being a bully. It is a case of top-down bullying. You are the bully's boss. Managers in your position uniformly fail to help. It is as if there is an invisible operational code that compels a manager's support for (actually, defensiveness on behalf of) his or her supervisor, regardless of the demonstrable facts in the situation.

It's especially tough when the alleged bully is Bob, your favorite supervisor. But if a target asks you directly for relief, your responsibility, your duty, is to ensure a safe workplace for that person. That should supersede the ties between anyone and Bob, the bully. Gather the facts. Don't get defensive on behalf of Bob.

Third-party complaints are vexing, too. Retaliation occurs in nearly every case where a complaint or lawsuit is filed. Therefore, you would be putting the target at risk even though your intentions to stop the bullying through a formal complaint process are honorable. The target should be the one to weigh the cost-benefit ratio and decide accordingly for himself or herself. The target bears the ultimate responsibility for filing a personal claim, not you.

Rather than coercing the target to file a complaint, just invite the person to talk while you listen without judgment. You are there solely to provide clarification and validation, if requested. The power of just "being heard" may be a sufficient salve for the emotional wound that may be temporary. No further action may be required. If the targeted employee wants to file a complaint later, follow the steps described previously. Of course, keep what you hear confidential. Do not start or contribute to a rumor.

Manager Step 3: Stop Rumors

Speaking of rumors, ethical, antibullying managers never start, pass along, or embellish them. The preferred action is to stop them when you hear them. Tell the last sender that you never want to hear those messages again. If the rumor involves your work team, make the slander a discussion topic at a team meeting. Make it a "teachable moment." Emphasize how hurtful rumors can be, and clear the air by declaring what you know to be true. Clarify your expectation about rumors and your disdain for people who initiate or sustain them. Equate initiating rumors with insults, degradation, and unacceptable bullying.

Rumors are not innocent communication channels. Gary was expert witness in a lawsuit involving the Los Angeles Police Department in which a 20-year veteran officer had her career stunted by a rumor that had dogged her at every promotion evaluation since leaving the police academy as a rookie. Rumors can cause serious damage.

Manager Step 4: Hold Executives Accountable for Bullying

Executives can be held accountable, of course, only when there is a policy in place with enforcement procedures that incorporate a 360-degree approach. There must be a procedural provision that reprisal, aimed at the person reporting the higher-ranking offender, would be grounds for serious consequences such as demotion or termination of the executive. This type of strong language and clear standards is part of the commitment that only organizations genuinely seeking to eliminate bullying craft into their policy and procedures. Is your commitment that strong?

Ensuring accountability up the hierarchy will be found only in the rarest of American organizations.

The Special Case of Women Bullies and Their Women Targets

We want to convey a special warning to women managers. Please fight the urge to torment women subordinates. The media absolutely loved the finding from our 2007 WBI national survey that when the bully was a woman, she chose to target other women in 71 percent of the cases. Well, in 2010, the targeting of women rose to 80 percent (compared with men, who targeted women 46 percent of the time). It was as if only women were bullies. In fact, men still represent the majority (62 percent). However, clips from the film *The Devil Wears Prada* still depict women's cruelty to other women in the workplace. Woman-on-woman bullying represents 30 percent of all bullying, not even close to a majority, but it has received heightened attention.

We've attempted to understand why the woman-on-woman bullying phenomenon is so prevalent and so noteworthy. Here are some explanations:

A. It's in the workplace where aggression is rewarded. Women see this (if not better than men) and learn to abuse others to get ahead. In male-dominated organizations, where men hold all or most of the executive positions, women tend to adopt male sex types of behavior to survive and succeed. Woman-on-woman bullying belies the popular stereotype of women as less aggressive, more dignified, and more respectful than men. It's counterintuitive.

B. A double standard about women is alive and well and practiced by both men *and* women. If women are "nice," they are too soft. If they are tough, they are "bitchy."

There are two social psychological explanations for why this occurs. First, there is gender bias in the causal attribution process. Causal attribution is simply showing a preference for explaining things that happen. Decades-old research found that if a person is described as succeeding at a task, the explanation depends on whether the person described is male or female. Success for men is typically explained by a trait, an inherent skill, intelligence, or ability. With exactly the same information, when it's a woman, success is described as the result of the task being so easy that anyone could have done it or it was simply luck. And both men and women elect those different explanations.

Second, the first person to break any historical organizational barrier, to be the lone representative of a group (and therefore in the statistical minority), is called a token. Tokens are subjected to disproportionate pressure. Errors, however tiny, are magnified. Successes can also be blown out of proportion. This is true for the first woman CEO or the first woman to attain a high rank in any organization or the first woman candidate for president. Women are tokens in male-dominated domains, like business. Men are rarely the only male in any role, but when they are, they too are tokens and heavily scrutinized.

C. Women targets are less likely to confront a person in response to being bullied. Targets of both genders rarely react with aggression. That's what makes them targets. Bullies sense an easier mark. Targets are sorted into those who take no action because of a higher moral calling or those who walk away in fear, stunned at the surprise attack. It could be religion that tells the first group to turn the other cheek or never to lower oneself to the level of a tyrant. For the other group, getting away is the only reaction they have. Once removed from the scene, they hope time will heal the wound or prevent it from happening again. Regardless of motive, targets do not defend themselves because either they are unable (it's not their worldview and they never acquired the skill of self-defense because it's a fair world and no one will hurt you) or they are unwilling to do so. Targets are all noncompetitive. It's not just women.

And women might possess another attribute likely to make them more susceptible to being targeted by bullies—they are high self-disclosers. In initial meetings, when first hired, eager-to-please individuals offer lots of information about themselves and their families in order to be "open" and friendly. The access to their inner lives backfires when the bully later uses that information to wound the target. Notice how bullies and those who crave power have a closed style and rarely reveal much. Not all women are open, but when they are, they make themselves vulnerable to a cunning bully.

D. Most bullies are bosses. All bullies prefer to bully subordinates. It's a prerogative that comes with the job that makes being a boss attractive to many people. So, bullying flows downhill. Women are bosses, too. But they are lower-ranking bosses than men bosses (only 15 percent of executives are women, and only 3 percent are CEOs). Therefore, they are more likely managing other women and not other men executives. They bully whomever they can. Women tormenting women may be based simply on proximity at work. One bullies those within reach.

E. Women are socialized to judge other girls while growing up as girls. They pay attention to how others look and dress all the time. Self-identity can be almost entirely dependent on how others appear.

Two factors emerge. First, modeling one's personal behavior on the actions of others gives a great deal of power to the other person. Clearly, in female-female relationships where apparent friendship preceded bullying, the target must have respected the bully. When the target is betrayed, she ruminates (for way too long) about the inexplicable turnaround, searching for a rational explanation. It doesn't matter; it's not rational—it just happened because the bully wanted it to. Second, the skill of paying attention since childhood determines the bully's perceptual field. For the bully, more information is gleaned from cultivating relationships with women. She notices how the others in the office act and dress and even how the others feel. In abusive, exploitative relationships, it is common for the dominant person to gather information from the abused for future use in attacks against the target. Targets fall into the trap easily.

F. Feminist writers claim that women grow up accustomed to having their personal boundaries invaded and thus learn to treat other women that same way. Some girls' opinions are treated as irrelevant by their fathers, whereas their brother's opinions are considered. A girl's ambitions are tamped down, expectations made more "realistic," and dreams treated as impossible. This is denial of her own psychological integrity, a discounting of her humanity. If this is how she is raised, she grows accustomed to being treated rudely or denigrated and as not deserving equal status with others. So, when bullied at work, her immediate reaction is rarely outrage and righteous indignation that another worker would dare lie so readily or be so unapologetically cruel. It is more likely a turning away, starting immediately to blame herself, buying into the lies (as if some "kernel of truth" is buried in all the manure), and spiraling into a psychologically compromised state. Read Phyllis Chesler's *Woman's Inhumanity to Woman*[33] for a thorough examination of this perspective.

11

Preliminary Steps to Address Workplace Bullying

Poor-Quality Partial Steps

Few organizations jump right into a comprehensive, systematic solution to stop workplace bullying. Most decision makers are timid and want to take small steps. Partial solutions range from the ineffective, which are covered first, to activities that after completion will justify longer-term solutions as the next step. Finally, we make the case for a broader, root-cause driven, systemic approach.

Approaches Based on the Bully's Personality

Three common "solutions" to the bullying problem are based on the "bad seed" model. The reasoning here is that you have only a few bad individuals, so if you fix them, you've solved the problem. Typical responses are to send the offender to one of the following:

- Communications skills training
- An anger management course or courses
- Remedial supervisory skills training

However, training is an inadequate answer—for several reasons. First, it generally fixes only deficiencies in skills. Furthermore, the trainee has to be willing to learn something new. Bullies already overestimate their personal capabilities and believe they can be taught little. Training, therefore, is a far from ideal way to handle them. And yes, some bullies *do* have anger issues. However, if the problem is the bully's prefrontal cortex (the brain area associated with impulse control), then no amount of training will mitigate it. Our system will change the environment to suppress emotional outbursts.

Remedial supervisory training is seen as punishment and could therefore backfire. Moreover, a majority of bullies bully because they lack the ability to manage others. They may, in fact, be so immature that a dearth of emotional intelligence prevents them from making genuine connections with the people they supervise. The key missing ingredients are empathy (an ability to adopt the viewpoint of another person and to share their emotional experience) and an accurate awareness of self (knowing actual versus desired skills and knowledge). It's highly unlikely that empathy can be taught.

Not all management training is good, because some curricula emphasize command and control and bolster *political* intelligence as most important. We do support enhanced skills training in how to manage others—provided that the leader takes time to review the curriculum screening for topics to enhance *emotional* intelligence.

Beware of Raising Employee Expectations Too Soon

This refers to the proper sequencing of introductory speeches and policy creation. Although educating people about bullying is a large part of our work, we discourage the practice of employers starting with "raising awareness" speeches. There are two unintended consequences. First, there will be a number of bullied individuals within the employee group, and such a message validates their experience (which, of course, is a good thing). They will feel believed for the first time and hear that they are not alone and that *they* did not cause the insufferable misery they endure. However—and this is where it gets complicated— they will also demand to know how you, the employer, will act on the bullying when they report it. Instead of raising awareness, you will be raising expectations that you are not yet prepared to satisfy.

The second problem with introducing an "awareness" initiative first is that you will alert bullies, who may escalate their detrimental behavior immediately after the speech to test the leaders' mettle. In short, they want to see if you dare stop them. They know that without a systemic solution under way, they face only the "bad seed"–training fixes. They've endured the training-as-punishment regimen before, and they can certainly do so again—and so the bullying continues unabated.

Positive Preliminary Steps to Take

There is a modified method of introducing the topic of bullying within the organization: measure the extent of bullying, then brief executives.

Prevalence Assessment

People in your organization who don't see bullying as a problem need you to convince them that indeed it is. They may be empiricists by nature, who don't believe anything unless they have experienced it, and are likely part of the 50 percent of the population in our 2010 Workplace Bullying Institute (WBI) national survey who have neither suffered nor witnessed bullying. You can't bully them simply to convince them, but you can assess prevalence and use it to provide the "proof" that they need. We make available—free to organizations of any size—an online survey to which all employees can be directed. Some survey items include:

- Our definition of workplace bullying to which the employee can claim knowledge as a current target or as a witness or report no knowledge of it in any way (allowing comparisons with the national prevalence rates of 9 percent, 15 percent, and 50 percent, respectively)

- Employees' perception of current safety from harm by psychological violence at work
- An estimate of confidence in their employer's current *ability* to stop bullying when reported using existing policies and procedures
- An estimate of confidence in their employer's current *willingness* to stop bullying when reported
- If bullying is experienced, an identification of the gender and rank of the principal perpetrators (and divisions within the organization—all while preserving the anonymity of respondents)
- Any additional questions that can assess the types of harm experienced (health, adverse employment decisions by managers, career, etc.)

As the antibullying project champion, you then can include the results in the internal proposal to start the dialogue about the demonstrably real problem on-site.

Executive Briefings

Executives must understand how bullying affects finances, reputation, and people, so it is best to educate them about workplace bullying. Administrators, trustees, directors, executives, and senior managers need to learn about the topic. A two-hour introduction (can they ever afford to spend more time?) can apprise them of the nature and extent of the problem within. You will also want to designate an internal champion to ensure commitment to a systemic solution.

Community Education

One helpful tactic is to offer a free seminar for the general public in your city. It is a nice adjunct to your internal education campaign, and it shows that your organization is thinking—and cares—about workplace bullying. The offering is good public relations. Of course, several of your employees will attend. They will approach HR with questions about the organization's commitment to which you can reply only that "preliminary exploration" is under way. Contrast this strategy with offering the introductory education in-house, thus incurring the wrath of those who have been waiting for action for years. This more subtle approach tends to provide a more natural launch to the program.

Making the Case for a Comprehensive Solution

Three core tasks lie ahead for leaders who have finished the preliminary work. They now know the extent of the problem. They have won support from the rest of the leadership team, and they have put bullies on notice that their reign of terror is about to end.

The Case for a Clear Line in the Sand: An Explicit Policy

Code of conduct violations and vague corporate values statements are not actionable—something that often surprises bullied targets. Policies, on the other hand, are entirely enforceable. In some states, they are considered a binding assurance from the employer to the employee. So the goal is to have a policy. Without one, bullies can argue successfully that their conduct is open to subjective interpretation. Bullies might claim that they are providing "training" for new employees, while the employees and witnesses describe how they were berated to the point of crying. Bullies assert that this is simply their "style" of coaching. Without a behavioral standard to which a bully's "style" can be compared, there can be no defensible accusation of wrongdoing. It's a moveable line that depends on the day when, and the person to whom, it is applied. This is why you must create a standard that cannot be misunderstood.

A New Unacceptability

The organization must send the message that misconduct that was once ignored or rewarded is now deemed unacceptable and prohibited. Bullies are frequently surprised to learn that behaving in ways that historically got them promoted could now be grounds for termination. It's a complete reversal of the norms that allowed them to terrorize others with impunity, as well as an upheaval of "the way we do things around here."

Of course, bullies will not accept this change calmly. They will test the new system to see if those responsible for the policy's enforcement have the political power and resolve to stop the omnipotent (at least in their minds) bully.

Enforcement Applies to All

We've been tough on executives with our candor that they need to stop coddling friends who are bullies. We even invited them to gauge whether or not they are the problem themselves. When a policy is applicable to all employees at all levels and ranks, the organization is saying that executives will be held accountable, too—something that can prove quite challenging. Board members' conduct should also be monitored and compared with the new policy's definitions of unacceptability.

Employees in management, as well as nonmanagers, will see the process as fair and credible when everyone faithfully enforces the policy. Executives will readily recognize the utility of having in place a system to prevent and correct bad conduct to which they refer when high-ranking bullies must be disciplined; after all, they can simply blame the impersonal "system." The bully completes a corrective action process, and the executive preserves his or her friendship with the bully.

12

A New Role for Human Resources

Executives mistakenly believe that like illegal harassment, workplace bullying is a problem for HR to solve. That is a traditional mistake. If your organization is to be successful at implementing our Blueprint system, HR will have a new role—one that involves the following 10 tasks.

1. **Gather evidence** about the prevalence of bullying by obtaining historical records of unactionable complaints from equal employment opportunity (EEO)/human rights/antidiscrimination officers.

2. **Consult with risk management** or the chief financial officer (CFO) to gather tangible losses attributable to bullying.

3. **Solicit a report** from contracted employee assistance program (EAP) counselors about the mental health impact of bullying on staff. Use aggregated stories to protect case anonymity.

4. **Assemble all related policies** (there will be many) to identify gaps that the new bullying policy will plug, thereby reducing redundancy across the myriad extant policies.

5. **Designate the members** of the collaborative policy writing group (which will be described in Blueprint Step 2) to be facilitated by the consultants. Coordinate logistics of this step.

6. **Coordinate internal education events** when it is time to roll out the new policy and procedures.

7. **Initiate and finalize the design** and production of ancillary materials to support the new policy and team of expert peers.

8. **Designate training team** participants (preferably with EAP providers) to receive in-depth education about the bullying phenomenon (either concurrently with preparation of the team of expert peers or as a stand-alone training).

9. **Identify and contract external investigators** to be available for cases when internal investigations of high-ranking offenders may be compromised.

10. **Train managers** to recognize signs of bullying and ways to intervene.

Despite what many people believe, HR should *not* direct the antibullying program—and here's why: according to former HR director Bruce Cameron in the documentary *Fired! The Movie*,[34] as well as Denise A. Romano's book *The HR Toolkit: An Indispensable Resource for Being a Credible Activist*,[35] HR professionals refer to themselves as the "Dark Arts" department. In addition, Yale Law lecturer and *Time* magazine writer Adam Cohen commented on our antibullying legislation during a segment on CNN-TV, during which he stated that HR is not on the workers' side in bullying situations.[36]

Consider the evidence. Since beginning this work more than 14 years ago, we have listened to 6,000+ hour-long sessions with workplace bullying targets. These telephone consultations have produced only two stories of HR bravery, courage, and morality—that is, of doing the right thing for the target and *not* for the bully. This is consistent with empirical evidence from the 2000 WBI survey of 1,300 targets, which suggests that HR did nothing in 51 percent of cases and actually *worsened* the situation for targets in 32 percent of cases. The bully's bosses were slightly worse (40 percent did nothing, and 42 percent increased the hurt). Although the findings came from a "nonscientific" study, the survey sampled people with the most direct experience in attempting to get help from HR and the bully's boss.

According to the 2007 WBI U.S. Workplace Bullying survey, of all adult Americans who witnessed or experienced bullying themselves, 44 percent said that employers (most likely an HR representative) did nothing when bullying was reported—and 18 percent said the employer made conditions worse. That was a large and scientifically representative sample. In a smaller WBI 2008 study, 40 percent of targets claimed that HR's investigations were "unfair or inadequate." With few findings in the targets' favor, bullies quickly learn that they can act with impunity (with 89 percent confidence, according to the WBI 2009 survey). No one can, or is willing to, stop them—certainly not HR, whose primary function is management support (and 72 percent of bullies are bosses).

The Society for Human Resource Management (SHRM), an HR trade association, opposes antibullying legislation called the Healthy Workplace Bill (HWB) in several states. When it becomes law, the HWB will hold individual offenders and employers accountable for repeated, malicious, health-harming abusive conduct perpetrated by bosses and coworkers. It is the official position of the HR industry to oppose a societal means of addressing workplace bullying. Clearly, HR is not a profession that advocates for employees.

Our online HR forum provided us with the following two anecdotal tales about the role HR played in situations experienced by two commentators.

Commentator 1
My bully in the workplace was the HR Director—[who was also] my boss. I was tormented for months until I finally resigned. It was awful. I called the ethics line that the company had in place and the CEO got involved. But since he backed the HR Director, there really was no place to go to complain.

Commentator 2

I was a Principal Scientist in the US for a major international corporation. My supervisor became upset when, at a project review meeting, I gave accurate and honest answers to questions about our competitive position on projects. I made it clear that I was not going to lie for him. He then harassed me for the next two years using the typical bullying tactics. I realized I would never be able to succeed under him and naively contacted HR, with the objective of reporting to a new supervisor. I was referred to an HR manager, [who] sent her a lengthy documentation of the harassment. She then proposed a mediated discussion with her, my supervisor, and me. I was surprised and elated that HR said my supervisor was amenable to it.

But the meeting never happened. Instead, the supervisor made an emergency visit to the US—and a few days later, my position was eliminated. The company's code of conduct states that each employee is entitled to be treated with respect, that abuses should be reported to HR, and that the company assures employees that it will take no action against employees that report abuse. After my dismissal, I arranged a meeting with two local HR people. They listened politely, and told me that I was not dismissed because of my complaint. Then, they warned me not to say bad things about their company and I never heard from them again.

Workplace bullying must be addressed by the organization's leader. It should not be delegated to the HR department to solve. When specific Blueprint steps are described, we will alert the reader to how to best use the HR department to support the antibullying project.

13

The Namie Blueprint to Prevent and Correct Workplace Bullying

Step 1: Assess

As the first step in assessment, it is important to quantitatively and qualitatively measure the current state of bullying at your organization.

Quantitative: How Bad Is It?

Gary is a veteran survey designer and university instructor of research methods and statistics. He has helped us create and post a survey customized for clients' needs at our private third-party data collection website. The prevalence in your organization can be compared against national estimates. Most importantly, preimplementation and postimplementation scores can be compared to gauge the antibullying initiative's efficacy. You should administer the postimplementation survey approximately six months after the launch of the new policy and procedures. We use an anonymous ID matching technique to allow for the strongest statistical analysis of the increase or decrease that results. We also suggest that you conduct periodic ongoing surveys to monitor project maintenance.

You can find some sample survey items in the section titled *Positive Preliminary Steps to Take* in Chapter 11.

Qualitative: What Is the Common Understanding?

For the qualitative audit, we interview designated individuals in private one-on-one sessions to determine the prevalence, manner, history, and consequences of bullying in the organization. The interviewees could be the bully's peers or managers. We gain a sense of the history, as well as receive specific examples of troubling incidents. Bear in mind that this is not a psychological review. Unless you have a licensed mental health professional with forensic experience on staff, the audit cannot be considered a psychological assessment, diagnosis, or treatment. It is merely a review of business processes and their impact on people and the organization. In return for candid participation, we require that executives guarantee that interviewees will be protected from retaliation.

Step 2: Create the Policy to Prevent Bullying

Creating the line in the sand that transforms misconduct previously tolerated or rewarded into unacceptable behavior is the cornerstone of the Blueprint system. When the leader tells the bully that the conduct must stop, it's easy for a bully operating in an organization without an explicit policy to challenge the authenticity of the leader's commitment. With no standard to which conduct can be compared, the bully can continue with impunity. Without a policy, cronyism and favoritism prevail.

A Collaborative Process

A single individual should never write a policy alone; it's far preferable to use a collaborative process. One advantage is that you increase the likelihood of designing a better policy with more relevant provisions based on the range of experiences a group brings to the task. Another, more important reason why the task should not be done in isolation is that everyone else in the organization is needed to help implement the policy when it is designated. People with no investment in the process will be hard to engage later. So for the sake of ownership, assemble a policy-writing group.

The group should include representatives from all divisions of the company: HR, risk management, legal, all unions, non-supervisory employees from a variety of functional departments, and management. Ideally, one member of the governing board should be invited to attend. You are to grant the group authority to write the policy and enforcement procedures, and no group or individuals should edit the group's work product.

Separate or Integrated?

The policy may be separate from existing policies or one that you integrate with the others. The advantage of a stand-alone policy is the weight and importance given to the goal of eradicating bullying. In short, it shows that you are serious about this initiative. Another benefit is that procedures unique to the new policy do not have to be affected by other policies. The disadvantage of a stand-alone policy is the risk of redundancies and overlap. For this reason, you'll want to assemble all the existing policies before you begin writing the new one. (This is HR task 4 in Chapter 12.)

Bullying, by definition, is harassment *not* based on protected status group membership. It is "status-blind" harassment. Therefore, policy provisions could supplement civil rights–related guidelines that prohibit a hostile work environment, gender harassment, and racial discrimination. The difficulty of integrating with these policies is that there are state and federal laws that compel employers to launch investigations whether or not the victim wants to file a complaint. The procedures to resolve bullying will always be different. Employers should be able to be flexible.

Bullying is also violence, albeit psychological violence. You could expand the antiviolence policies beyond the expressions of verbal abuse. In fact, bullying is often an assault with a threat of impending physical violence. It is not battery; it remains nonphysical. The integration with violence policies is superior to combining bullying with harassment policies.

Necessarily Idiosyncratic for Your Organization

You want to avoid boilerplate, tearsheet policies. Unless you take the time to customize the policy, it will become quickly inapplicable to specific circumstances. This will reduce it to an HR product that won't receive buy-in from anyone. We actually use a proprietary process to guide the policy-writing group to produce four deliverables: (1) the policy to address workplace bullying, (2) establishment of procedures to enable informal (before a complaint is filed) resolution of bullying incidents, (3) formal policy enforcement procedures to ensure personal and organizational accountability, and (4) the implementation plan and schedule from training to rollout.

Policies without enforcement always fail—so do not try to circumvent the process of developing enforcement procedures.

Step 3: Develop Informal Solutions

When formal complaints and investigations are the only options for bullied targets, trust in the new system will be low. Utilization will be predictably low because people justifiably fear retaliation. Informal resolution options provide the alternative to adjudication. Having an alternative may actually reduce the number of formal complaints, but that is not its purpose. It is to give options to bullied targets.

The Importance of a Precomplaint Process

Whereas other cultures, such as Scandinavian employers, for example, have 15 years or more of experience in dealing with workplace bullying, it's still a very new challenge to North American organizations. The U.S. workplace bullying movement began in mid-1997. It's understandable that organizations cannot be expected to go from zero awareness to having reliable resolution procedures in place immediately. For the sake of organizational learning, the policy-writing group needs to create ways for people who think they have been bullied to express their curiosity or doubts. They should not be required to file a formal complaint (thus avoiding the retaliation that nearly always accompanies complaint filing). Rather, they should be able to explore whether or not what is happening to them is bullying in the first place.

Clarification and Validation for Curious Employees

The best description of a bullied individual's initial response to a bullying incident is frozen inaction—like a "deer in the headlights." For most targets, the attack is the first in their working career. They are usually stunned and obsess over two questions: "How could the person be so cruel?" and "Why me?" It is a time of great confusion, not how to file a complaint.

Targets need to be listened to and given the opportunity to talk to someone about what is happening to them. Shame might even prevent some of them from taking the story home immediately. Someone at work needs to listen to help clarify the experience. It is important that they hear, "Yes, what you are going through seems to fit the organization's new antibullying campaign—and it is unacceptable." A validating message takes the form of, "You are not alone and did not cause this to happen. There are others to whom this happens. Go to the organization's website to read about it. It's called workplace bullying."

Clarifying and validating targets' experiences goes a long way in reducing their self-blame. The organization benefits by preventing premature, ill-conceived formal complaints that take time and use valuable resources. In most cases, "just being heard is enough" for targets. The generous act of kindness makes them feel less crazy and alone.

Who Will Serve Colleagues?

The policy-writing group answers this question. Whoever becomes the internal resource must develop a thorough understanding of the phenomenon, its impact on the organization and employees, and how traditional solutions actually tend to hurt, rather than help, bullied targets. In other words, employee health and safety must be paramount. You must determine who, or which group, in the organization is best suited to accomplish this task.

No Mediation!

One of dispute resolution professionals' favorite conflict resolution strategies is to rely on mediation by a neutral third party. However, mediation requires that you meet the needs and interests of both parties, and it is inextricably tied to HR-led solutions. HR often mandates that bullied targets participate with their bullies—and there is sufficient research that demonstrates that mediation is *not* the ideal solution for bullying.

Our colleague, Loraleigh Keashly, who serves as director of the Dispute Resolution Program at Wayne State University in Detroit, writes eloquently of mediation's shortcomings with respect to bullying.[37] For one thing, there is clearly a power imbalance in bullying cases; one person is a victim; the other is not. In addition, one party is unable to defend himself or herself—and because the targets were severely compromised beforehand, any attempt to meet "in the middle" actually reduces the target to even fewer resources. Furthermore, according to Keashly, mediation does not punish past behaviors, so the target can never win justice for the harm he or she has already suffered. Another criticism Keashly makes is that procedures are kept confidential, away from a public airing, which makes it impossible for other members of the organization to ever learn about evidence presented. Mediation prevents organizational progress in reducing the bullying.

Finally, bullying is a form of violence—and violence is not, and never should be, mediated. Mediation does not work for domestic violence cases, which is a close analogy of workplace abuse (see Appendix C). It sounds ludicrous to say to a battered spouse that the batterer has needs, too. Would you think it made sense to say, "Would it help if he only beat you three days a week?" No; it's ridiculous. The same is true for bullied targets. Do not further compromise those who have been compromised. In devising organizational solutions to bullying, it helps to honor the pledge to "Do No More Harm."

Step 4: Formal Enforcement Procedures to Correct Bullying

If leaders were to simply clone for bullying cases the enforcement procedures associated with antidiscrimination policies and laws, there would be a high level of distrust among employees. The historical role played by HR explains much of the distrust. That's why HR has new roles when the new policy is implemented.

Overcoming the "Sham Investigation" Tradition

According to a 2008 WBI online study that investigated employer responses to complaints about workplace bullying, only 8 percent of survey respondents believed there was a fair investigation, whereas 40 percent reported that the investigation was unfair. Two factors make an HR-led investigation "unfair," as perceived by bullied targets. First, there are no consequences of any kind for the perpetrator, and second, the target frequently receives retaliation for filing the complaint. Of targets in that survey, 40 percent lost their job as part of the retaliation.

Here's a personal account as posted on our online WBI Forum describing how haywire an investigation can go.

I became the target of a workplace bully in Jan. 2004 at the Respiratory Care Department of a medical center. [The bully's] behavior included withholding information that I needed to do my job, making false accusations about me, blocking communication, ostracism, and general rudeness. The evidence pointed to her disapproval of my religious and political beliefs as the cause for the bullying. I first reported the problem to the dept. manager in April. I made several more reports of the problem to department management in the following months, but nothing changed.

In December. I was diagnosed with PTSD [post-traumatic stress disorder] as a result of the bullying. I reported the PTSD injury to management but received no response. I scheduled a meeting with an HR manager in Jan. 2005. Even before he met with me, the manager indicated in an e-mail that he was not interested in hearing my side of the story. At the meeting during which was scheduled by me to report the problem, the HR manager did most of the talking. At the meeting's close, he said that he would meet with the bully and "get some answers to your questions." I waited a month, made an inquiry, waited another 2 weeks—and still received no response. All the while, the problem continued.

In May, I met with the HR manager again. This was in the middle of an "investigation" he was conducting into the problem I was having. He had spoken to approximately 20 co-workers who were aware of the problem. A few spoke to me about the HR manager's investigation and reported what they had told him. However, the information I received from HR was noticeably different. At that meeting he promised me that I would not have to work with the bully anymore. He also promised a written report of the investigation and a signed agreement that the bully and I [would] treat each other with respect if our paths crossed. I never received the report or the agreement, and the bully was scheduled to work with me in two months.

At the meeting, the HR manager accused me of having a personality change, that people had told him I was "not the fun person to work with" I used to be. That is certainly a typical change any victim of chronic bullying will experience; however, the tactless and heartless HR manager acted as if the personality change was my own fault. In July, I sent an e-mail to the department. The department manager responded by claiming that my injuries (PTSD) were "petty"—and the HR manger responded by threatening to fire me.

I had a third meeting with the HR manager in October. At that meeting, red-faced and bellowing at me across the room in a cramped office, he ordered me to lie about the PTSD injury if anyone asked, threatened to fire me if I talked about the bullying with anyone in the dept. or if I reported any more problems with the bully to anyone in management. He read a list of the false charges against me. I asked for a copy of them so I could respond. He refused. I asked for a copy of the report from his first investigation. Again, he refused.

I quit in August of 2006 after 30 years there, having always received excellent work evaluations. After leaving, I did what any responsible employee and citizen would do. I reported by mail and e-mail what happened to me and why I was leaving. My former employer reacted in a fury, falsely accusing me of threatening to harm either myself or others and had me involuntarily admitted to their psychiatric hospital.

Since I left, the bully and the department manager both received significant promotions. The extremely toxic HR manager has been there for over 35 years. It's my impression that this HR manager admires bullies because he is one.

Fair and Credible Processes

Employees are the judges of procedural fairness and credibility. Although management and HR may think they are doing a good job, they are more likely defending managerial prerogative rather than pursuing truths. Key changes to traditional investigations should include the following:

- Honoring deadlines, by complainants and investigators
- Expanding the evidence-gathering scope to facilitate drawing causal inferences based on preassault and postassault differences in targets' performance
- Including data about alleged prior allegations by taking into account pattern and practice and any history of chronic abusiveness

- Putting the onus of proof on the accused to show that he or she did not violate the policy as alleged
- Automatically registering a second complaint if retaliation of the complainant followed the initial filing
- Developing a method of registering complaints that failed to lead to confirmed violations of the policy and prohibiting the abuse of the policy enforcement procedures to bully an employee by false accusations
- Notifying the complainant and the accused about the investigator's decision and chosen remedies
- Creating innovative resolutions that restore employee health, lost economic status, and psychological safety for all workers who experienced incidents of bullying

Step 5: Provide Restorative Justice

The perception of injustice feeds targets' feelings of despair and hopelessness. It is important that the new policy and procedures address healing. Targets are wounded employees, impaired workers, through no fault of their own. Conscientious employers need to make them and the others who witnessed the incidents whole again.

For Bullied Employees

There are several aspects of bullying that are unjust. One of these is the unfair investigations that can lead to perceptions of procedural injustice by targets. Victims of bullying often believe that that system is stacked against them. They are seeking *retributive* justice when they attempt to identify violators and elicit the punishment they deserve for committing the violation. This type of justice is incorporated in formal policy enforcement procedures.

Ombudsman Tom Sebok at the University of Colorado at Boulder is an advocate for this kind of *restorative* justice for bullied individuals—something that we agree with entirely.[38] Justice depends on identifying (1) who has been harmed, (2) the nature of the harm suffered, and (3) how best to repair the harm. A restorative process looks for a solution that makes the target whole again. Sebok requires offenders to admit responsibility for the harmful conduct and to reflect on the adverse impact they had on bullied targets. Bullies who refuse to admit that they harmed others are not allowed to reharm their targets in any mediated or facilitated discussion with the target present.

The antibullying program would be undermined if too little attention were paid to the targeted individuals' need for justice. They do not simply want to "move on" and allow the bully to act with impunity; they want these bullies to acknowledge past transgressions in order to satisfy targets. Bullying in your organization will never be stopped unless perpetrators accept responsibility for their action.

The other key restorative process is *target healing*. Those being bullied should be separated from the perpetrators if they work in the same units and their paths inevitably cross. After an adequate healing time has passed, the target will have to return to work. You cannot expect this person to feel, or be, psychologically safe immediately upon return if he or she is forced to work under this same bully's thumb. And you certainly cannot expect the bullying to cease if there is no separation.

Transfers are potentially unfair when the only way to achieve safety for the target is to transfer him or her. Targets wonder why they should be forced to leave the job they loved and were good at performing when it was the bully who victimized them with a series of unsolicited and undesired attacks. This is why it's so important to devise a plan to ensure that target transfers don't seem like punishment.

For Witnesses

Witnesses are reluctant participants in investigations, and they experience a palpable fear of reprisal for helping targets. So when they do exhibit the courage to come forward with evidence, they deserve to be apprised of the investigation's outcome upon completion. They do not need to know the specific remedies or corrective actions; rather, they need to know whether or not the alleged policy violation was confirmed. When HR claims a confidential outcome is necessary to protect the bully, they are essentially saying that witnesses don't deserve the same protection—something that will make future witness cooperation much less likely.

Step 6: Deal with Confirmed Violators

Just as bullied individuals and affected witnesses need help, so do offenders. There's a hole in their soul somewhere. They deserve to explore their humanity again. We call the process our Respectful Conduct Clinic.

Not a Case of Zero Tolerance

An organizational culture shifts very slowly and reluctantly. With bullying—especially school-age incidences—schools jumped from zero awareness to zero tolerance in a single leap. However, everyone deserves a chance to show incremental changes and stay employed as we all learn and implement new strategies for dealing with others. Although zero tolerance policies are appropriate for some egregious instances of physical violence, workplace bullying should require at least two or three recorded, confirmed violations before the offender is terminated.

Peeling the Onion

We prefer to work with bullies on-site after they have been con-firmed as policy violators by the company's investigatory process. However, ideal timing is a luxury that organizations in pain do not always have. We are typically called in to ameliorate a crisis, usually one in which an over-the-top aggressive individual has gutted the organization's productivity and morale. Sometimes, we can attempt a short-term fix in which we quickly deal with the individual in question. However, our goal is always to concur-rently assemble the policy-writing group as soon as possible.

You can schedule meetings with the offender regardless of whether he or she is a confirmed policy violator. These should be conducted off-site for confidentiality purposes; even bullies deserve dignified treatment. There are three phases in the proj-ect we call the Respectful Conduct Clinic. It helps to have the services of a licensed mental health professional to deal with deep-seated psychological issues that may arise.

First phase: The chief executive officer (CEO) must man-date the offender's participation, and the offender's continued employment must rely upon attendance and cooperation. The early days of this process should be devoted to insight-driven inquiry into the offender's motivation to act in ways reported by coworkers (and sometimes customers). It's important to show empathy for the offender, because the pre-liminary task is to have the offender articulate why his or her unacceptable conduct happens.

Second phase: Self-discovery continues with testing and diagnostic instrument scoring, feedback, and interpretation of results. The goal of this phase is to discover the bully's personal barriers to change. Any skill deficiencies are iden-tified, and plans to reverse them are made. One of the sig-nature features of the clinic is that no change plans are made without an accompanying efficacy or impact metric. In other words, all changes are measured. There's no charm school training or anger management without a commensurate postintervention evaluation of the intervention's success. Evaluators should always be individuals ranked both above and below the offender.

Third phase: The focus switches from the offender as individual to offender as social actor in the work environment and, depending on her or his rank, on how the offender shapes the environment. At this point, you assess relationships and confront the offender with information about the impact of his or her actions. He or she must accept responsibility for the harm inflicted on others. Subordination of personal needs is coupled with a realignment of organizational and individual needs of those with whom the bully interacts regularly. The clinic ends with change-contingent contracting and a monitoring schedule that stretches two years into the future.

During the third phase, members of the consulting team confer with individuals at the workplace who were most adversely affected by the offender's misconduct. We train those individuals to recognize the renewal of toxic behaviors by the offender and to reward the offender for change if negative conduct ceases.

We do not delude ourselves into believing that offenders are immediately and permanently rehabilitated. That would involve personality change, which we know is highly unlikely. The best you can hope for is restraint and cessation of hostilities against other employees. The policy boxes offenders who are accustomed to roaming unfettered throughout the organization into a corner. The addition of consequences for bad behavior makes it an effort for bullies to behave in that manner. In the past, rewards came easily to bullies. With the policy and procedures in place—and if they are faithfully enforced—it soon becomes not worth the effort to behave badly given the new attendant risks. This stops most bullies, and their humanity returns. Only the psychopathic and truly disturbed ones carry on as if nothing has changed. The system eventually will snag and expel them—or they will quit, refusing to allow anyone to curb their impulsive behavior.

Step 7: Get the Word Out

Now that it's time to implement the new Blueprint system, the sophistication and completeness of all internal communications about the project should mirror the details of the system itself. Do not make this large investment and not ensure that every employee knows what it is and how to access team services. Do not let this become a binder-buried initiative.

Education about the Policy and Procedures

A cadre of employees is trained to educate all employees using a short (90-minute to 3-hour) rollout module. The all-hands education covers the rationale for the policy, its key features, and procedures written by the policy-writing group for achieving informal solutions and handling formal complaints.

Announcement of Team Services

Volunteers who care about workplace bullying are the ideal group to conduct training and to engage in empathic listening to individuals who are not certain they have been bullied. These individuals can be trained to be more expert in the topic than other employees. Thus, they become the go-to team who can help colleagues.

A Shift in the Paradigm to an Employee Health Focus

It won't be easy to accomplish a culture change, because bullying is woven into the fabric of all capitalistic and militaristic organizations. It is not remarkable that bullying happens; for countless companies, it is simply "the way we do things here." There is tremendous pressure to maintain the status quo. However, if you have read this far, you are optimistic that you can start an anti-bullying effort where you work. The pushback will not tear down systems in place.

Instead, you have only to argue for maximizing employee health. It makes good business sense to prevent the needless stress-related diseases attributable to a bullying-prone workplace culture. The new focus on a distress-reduced, bullying-free workplace is a strong positive force. Empathy, healing, justice, fairness, and accountability will make the work world right for the vast majority of employees and will restore optimism in the belief that the world can again be a benevolent place. Your employees and colleagues will be grateful to you for voluntarily launching this initiative.

Step 8: Optimize Accountability

True culture change requires the indoctrination of the antibullying spirit in *every* aspect of workplace life.

Integration with Performance Evaluations

If the desirable conduct is important to you and your organization, then you absolutely have to measure it. You can catch unacceptable conduct by using the appraisal system. Add the dimension of managing without resorting to abusive conduct as a metric that contributes to the determination of bonuses, pay raises, or the ability to be promoted. For good measure, ask nonsupervisory employees to evaluate their supervisors' and managers' conduct regarding respectful treatment of others, regardless of rank.

New Hiring Strategies

As discussed before, searching for ambitious managers can lead to a staff full of bullies. Start inquiring about how well applicants managed others by gathering opinions from the people they managed. Making reference checking a bosses-only tradition means that you're talking to the probable sponsor of an aggressor who admired her or his style. Managers have customers of their management services; they are called subordinates, and they can verify the person's level of managerial skill. We suggest you reference check subordinate staff at the employer's workplace prior to the one at which he or she now works. Those staff members will speak most honestly and freely.

The more expert at the work the manager is, the less likely he or she is to use bullying as a cover for the lack of knowledge or insecurity. Try to minimize hiring managers to manage outside their technical areas.

Modified Management Training

After covering the basics, you might want management training to include a section on how to recognize bullying in peers. Intervention strategies, as discussed back in Manager Preparation (step 2) in Chapter 10, should be taught. The new policy will preserve managers' right to discipline employees. In exchange, there should be added a new responsibility to monitor the workplace for bullying incidents and to intervene when possible. At the very least, supervisors must intervene on behalf of bullied victims within their units when relief is requested of them.

Redefinition of "Success," Starting with Orientation

When you announce the new policy, procedures, and support services, most employees will respond enthusiastically. Some veteran cynics will not believe leadership's commitment and might root for the effort to fail and revert to a dispensable "fad of the month." By contrast, the most hopeful audience for the antibullying message will be new hires. Include in the orientation a clear module—perhaps a video of the rollout education from the initial launch—explaining how employees are expected to conduct themselves in alignment with the policy and procedures.

14

Sustain the Bully-Free Culture

Avoiding Trips and Traps in the Future

Congratulations! You made it to the other side of the mountain. It was uphill as you struggled to win support for the antibullying project. Several powerful forces were aligned against you, but you prevailed. That's the good news. The bad news is that you cannot afford to relax. According to the Blueprint plan, you should have a team of antibullying ambassadors in place to share the burden of maintaining momentum.

Some of the jerks, weasels, and snakes (J-W-S) who were the reasons for the project in the first place are still lurking. They are personally offended. Their goal now is to torpedo the policy and challenge its enforcement.

Here are some of the things that go awry in the postimplementation phase:

- The J-W-S will attempt to have one of their allies or minions put in charge of policy enforcement.
- The J-W-S will flood the system with frivolous complaints but will follow rules to the letter so that detection is difficult.
- The J-W-S will try to convince the executive team to scuttle the entire project.
- The J-W-S will pretend to be rehabilitated and volunteer to be on the peer team so as to undermine its effectiveness.
- The J-W-S will wait for a change in executives and then lobby the new person to abandon the project.
- One of the J-W-S will become the next executive and kill the project.

Train Interveners and Encourage Altruism

Bullied individuals lament that neither witnesses nor coworkers do anything to stop the incidents of humiliation and intimidation. We discussed some of the reasons for inaction in Chapter 7. To sustain antibullying progress, someone or some group will have to step up to intervene.

The Science of Bystander Nonintervention

We previously discussed the scientific studies about why bystanders fail to act in emergencies. Factors that reduce the tendency to help include fear; overestimation of personal risk; situations that are vague and ambiguous; the inaction of others, which convinces people to do nothing; personal feelings that it might be inappropriate to intervene; identification more with bully than target; and the diffusion of responsibility that comes from believing many others could also help so surely one of them will help.

To counter these factors, there must be training for everyone about how to help others. Some of our clients write into their policies an obligation for every employee to respond when they witness any bullying. Other clients hold only managers responsible.

The alternative to a requirement to help is designating the task of intervening to a special group of employees. Everyone in the organization would know the group members. The members become the "official" interveners. It is critical that the group have members representing all ranks in the organization. No nonsupervisory employee should be made to intervene in bullying incidents involving executives.

Safe Intervention Strategies

The framework for types of interventions is simple: two factors with two categories each. One factor is timing, real-time or delayed. Will the interveners be there at the instant when bullying happens? This is easy when in meetings with the bully. Otherwise, most interventions have to be delayed whether they were witnessed or not. The other factor is personal risk to the intervener, high or low.

The riskiest interventions are the ones undertaken immediately, during the incidents, and involve high-risk actions. A bully is screaming at the target in the hall when you happen to pass. In real-time and with high risk, you, the intervener, thrust yourself between the two and defend the target. (Can you see your Superman cape flying in the breeze as you rush to the victim's rescue?)

It need not be so dramatic, even in real time. An intervener need only approach the target, gently grab his or her arm, and escort the person away, saying only "please come with me." The fact that you would be known as a designated intervener in your role with the antibullying team would protect you. The bully might protest to your manager later, but your role would protect you.

The antibullying group would develop intervention strategies appropriate to use within the organization. The majority of interventions turn out to be delayed and low risk. The group would then educate all staff about what to expect. As employees grow accustomed to the work of the group, the culture shifts from tolerance of bullying to intolerance. The group is the catalyst for that transformation.

Don't Allow Antibullying to Become "Fad of the Month"

Employers commonly commit to large projects and spread them far and wide across divisions until the entire organization is blanketed. Despite the wide distribution, the commitment is paper-thin. There is no credible enforcement in some places.

No teams have been trained. And authoritarian managers cling to old ways for fear of losing control. Plant deep roots in every corner of your organization. Make it stick.

A New, Rational Place

The antibullying effort can be prevented from becoming a dispensable fad. It takes time to build the record of employee satisfaction with both the informal and formal resolution procedures. The first formal test of the system is most critical. It must be perceived as fair and free from interference.

As time passes, bullies will quit rather than be held accountable. Some will be censured and abandon their destructive practices. The organization can celebrate its antibullying champions and ambassadors. Eventually, the reward system—who gets promoted, who gains recognition—is rebalanced. The J-W-S fade into obscurity, and the good people become prominent.

Bullying makes the workplace an irrational and scary place to spend your waking hours. With a successful Blueprint implementation, rationality and safety are restored (or put in place for the first time if never a part of the culture before). Over time, "culture" changes for the better, rendering bullying an antisocial behavior.

One Step Ahead of the Law

In 2010 the Healthy Workplace Act passed in the senate in both the New York and Illinois state legislatures. The bills addressed workplace bullying by prohibiting repeated, health-harming, malicious abusive mistreatment by anyone in the states' workplaces. In New York, the senate passed S 1823-B and came within a day of voting for its passage in the relevant Assembly Labor Committee. In Illinois, SB 3566 was passed in the senate. Only rancor between the house speaker and the governor over the bill kept it from reaffirming an early house committee vote for passage.

As of April 2011, the Healthy Workplace Bill (HWB) had been introduced in 21 state legislatures. Canada has four provincial and one federal regulation addressing bullying. All other Western industrialized nations have laws. It is only a matter of time before U.S. employers will be compelled to prevent and correct bullying.

Soon, states will enact laws addressing workplace bullying. Many corporate employment lawyers blog prolifically during the legislative season. They warn their clients to track progress of the HWB. The lawyers tend to oppose a law that could hold their clients responsible for malevolent conduct. However, they strongly suggest that organizations *voluntarily* adopt a program like the one we detailed in this book because it makes good business sense.

Our Blueprint also gives your organization an exemption from the HWB when it becomes law. Contained in the bill are several affirmative defenses for employers. The main one is a provision granting freedom from vicarious liability for the actions of a malicious, abusive, health-harming employee. To qualify, you need only have a policy and enforcement procedures in place and use them. Implementing our Blueprint precludes your liability.

You can track progress of the HWB as it moves toward enactment at healthyworkplacebill.org.

Build Your Bullying-Free Workplace Brand

At this time, our Blueprint to prevent and correct workplace bullying is the gold standard in the industry in the United States. We hope that by adopting it, you and other adopting organizations will be able to claim to be free of workplace bullying. We plan a future certification process for clients with demonstrated sustainable results and momentum.

We know that you can win the competition for recruitment and retention of the most talented employees on the market. And we are certain that bullying-free organizations should be able to be most effective in the marketplace of products and services with your competitors. Bullying-free workplaces have high worker engagement because employees are free to focus on the work and to ignore the politics. The organization protects employees.

After you have implemented the Blueprint system, brag about it. It makes for good public relations. There is a long tradition of corporate social responsibility (CSR) that adopters have exploited for organizational benefit. With the antibullying campaign, you have turned inward and acted with social responsibility toward your employees. In many ways, the initiative is more authentic than most CSR projects.

Review your organization's CSR record. Ask your communications and public relations staff how to catapult your organization into prominence for having successfully implemented our Blueprint system. Ask your employees. Their gratitude for having stopped the bullying will give you ideas about how to position your organization.

The media repeatedly ask us when employers are going to voluntarily stop workplace bullying. They are eager to feature early-adopting organizations. The public relations task will be easier than you imagine.

Are you ready to make news? We can help.

Appendix A
Macro-Bullying Trends That
Make Workers Dispensable

Taken together, the four trends described in this appendix define the 21st-century employment landscape and coarsen our society. In turn, organizational behavior is embedded in that society. The workplace culture is inseparable from the best and worst of how we behave on a larger scale with fellow human beings.

Through the steps of our Blueprint program, you will be humanizing the workplace to offset the chilling effects on surviving workers. Describe the project as a deserved benefit to workers. This is not a lie.

Globalization

If you work for a global multinational corporation, the recent (and into the foreseeable future) practice of hiring the lowest paid workers in the world connotes the corporation's disregard for the worth of individuals. Driving wages to their lowest levels deprives people of the ability to own a home, raise and feed a family, afford life-sustaining health care, educate their children, and live a retired life in relative safety and comfort. If you have internalized that attitude of disregard the employer embraces, you will find it difficult or impossible to stop workplace bullying within the company.

It's also noteworthy that multinationals operating around the world must follow the labor laws in host nations. In the Canadian provinces of Quebec, Ontario, Saskatchewan, and Manitoba, employers with bullying employees face legal repercussions. The same is true in Australia, Britain, Ireland, France, Germany, Finland, Sweden, Norway, Belgium, and even Serbia! In fact, in the rest of the Western industrialized world, laws exist to curb workplace bullying, which may be known in those countries as mobbing, psychological harassment, or moral harassment. These widely dispersed employers know how to comply with stricter labor regulations. The reason they do not have to do the same in the United States is because there are no such regulations.

Privatization of the Public Sector

If you work for government at any level, there are austerity pressures to cut everything from supplies, services offered, and the labor force. U.S. federal civilian workers were slapped with a two-year pay freeze in December 2010. There is a common misperception that public employees enjoy undeservedly lavish compensation. It is a myth that is so widespread that private sector workers believe it about their counterparts. A 2010 report from the Political Economy Research Institute at the University of Massachusetts[39] debunked the myth. High-wage workers in state and local government (in New England, where the survey was conducted) earn 13 percent less than their private sector counterparts when taking into account age and education. Middle-wage workers earn an average of 3 percent less. Government workers do have better sick leave and health insurance benefits, but most other benefits are equivalent to those in the private sector. In 2010, 37 percent of government workers were unionized.

Government jobs were once exclusively performed locally and only by workers on the payroll. Peter Drucker, management guru, coined the term *privatization*. Local services at the City of Lakewood, California, a city with population 70,000, has 177 employees on the payroll because most of their city services are contracted out. Other cities adopting the concept include Indianapolis, Phoenix, Akron, Kansas City, Minneapolis, New Orleans, Oklahoma City, and Charlotte.

The "spoiled" government workers myth can invade a manager's consciousness. It can create a bias that potentially interferes with routine interactions at work. Here's how: The stereotype suggests that workers in government are slackers, unmotivated, and less talented than employees in corporations. Through such a negative lens, it is easy to see individuals as not deserving respect, task assistance, or managerial support. The myth facilitates bullying of an entire labor force—federal, state, province, county, region, or municipality workers.

Commoditization of Labor

In our contemporary economy, more and more things are considered commodities. Originally used to describe an economic good that lacks a qualitative or product or brand differentiation across markets, *commodity* referred to resources and agricultural products such as salt, sugar, coffee beans, rice, aluminum, copper, gold, silver, and crude oil. Commodities are bought and sold on worldwide exchanges for profit. Industrial extraction companies scour the globe in search of the cheapest supplies in order to maximize profits.

Merriam-Webster dictionary also defines people as commodities when "subject to ready exchange or exploitation within a market." And so workers have become commodities. Corporations search the globe for workers willing to work for the lowest wages. Local workers are dispensable. Community unrest follows economic crisis after local employers with a large number of employees displace them all by shipping jobs overseas.

American high-paying technology jobs moved to China and India, where employees worked for a tiny fraction of U.S. wages. Taiwan fulfills manufacturing contracts by offshoring jobs to China. Nearly all U.S. manufacturing jobs were sent to China decades ago. German and Japanese auto manufacturers were enticed to build plants in states throughout the U.S. South with no-tax policies and access to inexpensive, nonunion workers. Within 30 years, the American tradition of hiring third-world workers has come full circle. Now it is the American workers who are easily exploited.

From this trend toward making workers commodities, there are three important outcomes. First, the outsourcing company is exploiting inexpensive workers. Outsourcing itself is a degrading, dehumanizing process. It shows disrespect for workers by nationality because they can be so easily and cheaply contracted. Second, the process tells local workers that they do not deserve work, that they are dispensable. They are unworthy because they require a wage sufficient to live in the country of their birth. Third, when we treat fellow human beings as market commodities, we have lost our moral authority to demand dignity for ourselves. Why should anyone be allowed to deny dignity for others?

Elimination or Prevention of Unions

The only way for workers to offset in any way the power imbalance between owners and workers is to unionize to pursue collective bargaining. Otherwise, workers operate as individuals without aggregate power when disputes arise with the employer about work conditions.

As we write this, only 7.2 percent of private sector civilian workers in the United States belong to a union. When public sector employees are included, the total unionization rate is approximately 12 percent. Union density was highest in the United States in 1945, when 36 percent of workers were in unions. Membership *rates* declined from 1983 to 2008, the *numbers* are the lowest since the 1940s. The United States has the lowest rate among the rich countries: Finland and Sweden, both above 70 percent; Denmark, Norway, Iceland, and Greenland, all above 60 percent; Ireland, 32 percent; Canada, 28 percent; United Kingdom, 27 percent; Germany, 20 percent; Japan, 18 percent; and Korea, 10 percent. All of the nations except those in Scandinavia are shrinking the proportion of workers who are unionized. Workforce reductions in response to the Great Global Recession of 2008 among governments are diminishing unions. Privatization and outsourcing of public services also cut the size of unions.

The most famous private sector corporation to fight unionization is also the world's largest, with 2.1 million employees— Wal-Mart a store. An American management memo about the corporation's opposition to unionization from one of its managers was leaked. We found it on the Internet. The messages contained therein reveal a contemptuous attitude toward Wal-Mart workers in general and especially workers who dared to consider dignity at work a personal right. Here's the slightly abridged memo with no changes to the remaining text.

> As a member of Wal-Mart's management team, you are our first line of defense against unionization. This toolbox will provide you with valuable information on how to remain union-free in the event union organizers choose your facility as their next target.

Early warning signs:

- Increased curiosity in benefits
- Associates receiving unusual attention from other associates
- Associates talking in hushed tones to each other
- Abuse of rest-room visits
- Associates spending an abnormal amount of time in the parking lot before and after work

Types of Associates Attracted to Unions

Unions have learned to identify certain types of individuals who are more susceptible to union exploitation than others:

1. The "inefficient associate" realizes that he or she will not be able to measure up to the facility's standards and will be terminated. This person is attracted to the union because they convince the worker that they will clothe him or her with the so-called shield of job security.
2. The "rebellious associate" is attracted to the union cause simply because he or she is opposed to all management or bosses. This person consequently becomes an antagonist to the employer and a respondent to the union propaganda.
3. The "something-for-nothing associate" is the typical injury faker who has collected workers' compensation from most former employers. This person is always looking for a deal and takes every imaginable shortcut in the job, sincerely believing that the world owes him or her a living.
4. The "chronically dissatisfied associate" might be one of the most productive associates, but he or she will find fault with everything. This person is a hopeless griper, as distinguished from a constructive critic. A truly

unhappy individual, the chronically dissatisfied associate was probably born unhappy, is going to die unhappy, and is going to be unhappy for the duration between.

5. The "cause-oriented associate" will jump on any bandwagon that passes through the area. This is the same individual who joined all the "off-beat" organizations in high school or college, such as taking a trip to India to visit his or her personal "guru."

6. The "overqualified associate" is out of his or her element. This person might well be a PhD operating a grinding machine or a former accountant sweeping the floor, but his or her station in life has deteriorated to the point that personal vanity suffers. The overqualified associate will attempt to exert influence over his or her fellow associates in an effort to bolster a deflated ego and will be attracted to the union simply because the union will seem to offer hopes of returning to his or her previous station in life.

Staying union free is a full-time commitment. Unless union prevention is a goal equal to other objectives within an organization, the goal will usually not be attained. No one in management is immune from carrying his or her "own weight" in the union-prevention effort. Unless each member of management is willing to spend the necessary time, effort, energy, and money, the Wal-Mart union-free objective will not be accomplished.

Canadian unions, however, are making progress. The first Wal-Mart union was established at a store in Jonquiere, Quebec, in 2005 that the company shut down when ordered to negotiate with workers after a successful election. In 2008, workers at a Wal-Mart Tire & Lube shop in Gatineau, Quebec, voted to unionize, and the company shut down that store as well. In

2010, back in Gatineau, another union election was held and 150 workers won the right to be represented. A Wal-Mart store in Saint-Hyacinthe now has a contract with UCFW Local 501.

In Weyburn, Saskatchewan, the struggle to unionize has been a drawn-out process. It started with a vote to be unionized in 2004. Certification in 2008 was followed by countless appeals by the corporation. It ended with a Supreme Court decision on October 14, 2010, upholding the union's right to represent the workers. Wal-Mart was ordered to move forward and negotiate a contract. To date, there are three unions in place in Wal-Mart Canada, none in the United States.

Appendix B
The Namie & Namie Bibliography

Publications

Namie, G. "Framing the bullying revolution's message." Keynote address given at the 7th International Conference on Workplace Bullying & Harassment, Cardiff, Wales, UK, June 2010.

Namie, G., & Lutgen-Sandvik, P. (2010) Active and passive accomplices: The communal character of workplace bullying. *International Journal of Communication*, 4, 343–373.

Namie, G., Namie, R., & Lutgen-Sandvik, P. (2010) Challenging workplace bullying in the USA: A communication and activist perspective. In S. Einarsen, H. Hoel, D. Zapf, & C. Cooper (Eds.), *Workplace Bullying: Development in Theory, Research and Practice (2nd edition)*. London: Taylor & Francis.

Namie, G., & Namie, R. (2009) *The Bully at Work* (2nd edition). Naperville, IL: Sourcebooks.

Namie, G., & Namie, R. (2009) U.S. workplace bullying: Some basic considerations & consultation interventions. *Journal of Consulting Psychology*, 61(3), 202–219.

Lutgen-Sandvik, P., Namie, G., & Namie, R. (2009) Workplace bullying: Causes, consequences, and corrections. In P. Lutgen-Sandvik & B. D. Sypher (Eds.), *Destructive organizational communication: Processes, consequences, and constructive ways of organizing*. New York: Routledge/Taylor & Francis.

Namie, G. (2008) Create a blueprint for a bullying-free workplace. *The Complete Lawyer, Vol 4*(1), online at www.thecompletelawyer.com.

Namie, G. (2007) The challenge of workplace bullying. *Employment Relations Today, Vol 34*(2), 43–51.

Namie, G., & Namie, R. (2005) Workplace bullying in healthcare. *Clinician News, Vol. 9*(11), 14–15.

Namie, G., & Namie, R. (2004) Workplace bullying: How to address America's silent epidemic. *Employee Rights and Employment Policy Journal, Vol. 8*(2), 315–333.

Namie, G. (2003) Workplace bullying: Escalated incivility. *Ivey Business Journal*, a publication of Ivey Business School, University of Western Ontario, Canada.

Namie, G., & Namie, R. (2003) Anti-bullying advocacy: An unrealized EA opportunity. *Journal of Employee Assistance, Vol. 33*(2), 9–11.

Namie, G., & Namie, R. (2000) Workplace bullying: Silent epidemic. *Employee Rights Quarterly*, Autumn, 2000.

Namie, G., & Namie, R. (1998) *BullyProof Yourself at Work*. Benicia, CA: DoubleDoc Press.

Research Studies

2011: Unions and Workplace Bullying. Online, n=313

2010: Employer Engagement with Workplace Bullying. Online (n=332) vs. nat'l sample (n=2,658)

2010: Education and Workplace Bullying, n=4,210

2010: The U.S. Workplace Bullying Survey. Workplace Bullying Institute–Zogby International authoritative scientific nationally representative sample of adult Americans, n=4,210

2009: The economic crisis and bullying/WBI Summer 2009 Survey. Online, n=300

2009: (Still) Bullying with impunity/WBI Labor Day 2009 Survey. Online, n=422

2008: WBI survey of employer responses to workplace bullying. Online, n=400

2008: WBI survey of coworker responses to workplace bullying. Online, n=400

2007: The U.S. Workplace Bullying Survey. Workplace Bullying Institute–Zogby International authoritative scientific nationally representative sample of adult Americans, n=7,740

2003: WBI Report on Abusive Workplaces. Online, n=1,000

2000: WBI U.S. Hostile Workplace Survey. Online, n=1,335

Appendix C
Bullying Is Domestic Violence
when the Abuser Is on Payroll

In so many ways the two phenomena uncannily mirror each other. With bullying and partner violence, the abuser's motive to control and dominate the victim starts the process and determines the nature and extent of the sick, twisted relationship that follows. The perpetrator objectifies the victim. In 98 percent of domestic violence cases, the perpetrator is male. In bullying, the majority of abusers, 62 percent, are male, although women are perpetrators, too. Regardless of gender, the bully-abuser dehumanizes his or her prey. The bully-abuser can have such contempt for the target that he or she refuses to grant even the minimal respect due to a fellow human being. Dehumanization enables the severe mistreatment. When the recipient is not seen as an equal, it is easy to denigrate, belittle, and humiliate. The target is a lesser-than object not deserving decent treatment.

The forms of mistreatment that accompany objectification can cause emotional harm. The digs are ad hominem attacks about the person's worthlessness and undeservedness. These assaults result in stress-related health harm, both physical and psychological. Emotional harm outlasts physical injuries that occur in domestic violence cases. Short of death, the abused spouse is likely to suffer more from emotional damage than from broken bones that heal relatively more quickly. The legacy of emotional torment, the traumatization, can last a lifetime after infliction. With bullying, there is no physical violence, only the emotional.

Another overlap between domestic violence and bullying is that friends close to the principals tend to distance themselves from abusive situations. This gives them cover to plausibly resist getting involved. Doing nothing becomes easier if they are not present when the abuse happens. Closest friends of the abuser tend to justify the actions. "He wouldn't hurt a fly." "When I'm with him, he is a gentle, kind soul." "She's absolutely brilliant, and because she doesn't suffer fools gladly, people working for her have to learn to adapt to her style."

Finally, institutions initially duck their responsibility to act. For years, domestic violence cases perplexed police officers called to homes during an abuser's attack, where the fearful victim would not agree to file charges, meaning nothing could be done. Now that criminal laws are in place, police can apprehend abusers when warranted, regardless of the victim's willingness to go along. Note that it took laws to allow law enforcement to intervene on behalf of injured and abused victims of domestic violence. It was not simply changing societal norms that reversed support for abusers that made the difference.

With respect to workplace bullying, employers, the institutions that host the abusers, loathe calling them what they are. They act like the rationalizing, back-peddling friends who want to say nothing bad about employees who do bad things to other employees. A former director of the historically dysfunctional Minerals Management Services (MMS) Bureau within the U.S. Department of the Interior said to us, when we recommended the forced termination of a demonstrably harmful bully division chief, "No, I won't do it because he is a great conversationalist and a lunch buddy." Well there you have it. No need to act; he wouldn't harm a fly.

But the evidence spoke otherwise. All employees in that division were stressed. Employees had suffered multiple heart attacks, strokes, and other cardiovascular complications from working for the bully. But friendship with the executive trumped all reason.

Years later, in 2010, when the BP oil platform exploded in the Gulf of Mexico and killed 11 workers and poisoned the environment, MMS made news. It was the agency whose employees (not the ones with whom we worked at Herndon, Virginia, headquarters) had had sex with oil and gas industry counterparts. MMS was corrupt. Its culture was corrupt when it allowed the bullying to damage so many lives for glib reasons stated by the inept director.

So, we ask, are laws required to compel employers to stop abusers on the payroll? It took laws to allow law enforcement, representing society, to disrupt domestic violence.

Notes

1. R. Wilson, "What killed Kevin Morrissey?" *Chronicle of Higher Education*, August 12, 2010.
2. Virginia Tech Review Panel. Mass shootings at Virginia Tech: Report of the Review Panel presented to Governor Kaine, August 2007.
3. H. Leymann, "Mobbing and psychological terror at workplaces," *Violence & Victims* 1990, 5(2), 119–126.
4. H. Leymann and A. Gustafsson, "Mobbing at work and the development of post-traumatic stress disorders," *European Journal of Work and Organizational Psychology* 1996, 5(2), 251–275.
5. A. Adams and N. Crawford, *Bullying at work* (London: Virago, 1992).
6. "Woman city worker wins £800,000 in Deutsche Bank bullying case," *Daily Mail* (London), August 2, 2006.
7. The NAQ Scale: S. Einarsen and B. Raknes, "Harassment in the workplace and the victimisation of men," *Violence and Victims* 1997, 12, 247–263.
8. P. Lutgen-Sandvik, S. J. Tracy, and J. K. Alberts, "Burned by bullying in the American workplace: Prevalence, perception, degree, and impact," *Journal of Management Studies* 2007, 44(6), 837–862.
9. P. L. Schnall, M. Dobson, and E. Rosskam (eds.), *Unhealthy work: Causes, consequences, cures* (Amityville, NY: Baywood Publishing, 2009).
10. R. M. Sapolsky, *Why zebras don't get ulcers*, 3rd ed. (New York: Holt, 2004).

11. E. S. Epel, E. H. Blackburn, J. Lin, et al., "Accelerated telomere shortening in response to life stress," *Proceedings of the National Academy of Science (PNAS)* 2004, 101(49), 17312–17315.

12. K. Williams, "Ostracism," *Annual Review of Psychology* 2007, 58, 425–452.

13. E. Dias-Ferreira, J. C. Sousa, I. Melo, et al., "Chronic stress causes frontostriatal reorganization and affects decision-making," *Science* 2009, 325(5940), 621–625.

14. Leymann, Mobbing and psychological terror.

15. S. B. Matthiesen and S. Einarsen, "Psychiatric distress and symptoms of PTSD among victims of bullying at work," *British Journal of Guidance & Counselling* 2004, 32(3), 335–356.

16. J. A. Richman, K. M. Rospenda, S. Nawyn, et al., "Sexual harassment and generalized workplace abuse among university employees: Prevalence and mental health correlates," *American Journal of Public Health* 1999, 89(3), 358–363.

17. The estimate of 2.9 million Americans losing their jobs because of bullying comes from the following formula using data from the 2010 WBI U.S. Workplace Bullying Survey. The percentage of those who quit to stop the bullying + the percentage terminated as a result of bullying = 36.7 percent. The percentage claiming to be currently bullied is 8.8 percent. The percentage of the entire sample that answered the specific question about what made the bullying stop is 38.9 percent. The size of the adult (older than age 18) population at the time of the survey was 231 million Americans. The formula used was as follows: $0.367 \times 0.088 \times 0.389 \times 231,000,000 = 2,902,086.264$.

18. H. Leymann and A. Gustafsson, *The Suicide Factory*. Published by Norstedts Juridik in Swedish in 1998 as *Självmordsfabriken*. The authors accessed a copy of the unpublished English language manuscript.

19. *Murder by Proxy: How America Went Postal*. Directed by Emil Chiaberi; produced by James Moll & Michael Rosen (Key Element Productions, 2009).

20. Indiana Supreme Court Case No. 49502-0710-CV-424, April 8, 2008.

21. *Clarion: The Newsletter of the Professional Staff Congress*, City University of New York, May 2005.

22. ACCLAIM Ability Management Inc., Toronto, Ontario, Canada, Tony Fasulo, Managing Partner.

23. The Great Place to Work® Institute produces the annual *Fortune* 100 Best Places to Work list, the membership of which is a coveted designation by participating businesses.

24. International Labour Organization, "New forms of violence on the rise worldwide," June 14, 2006, press release, Geneva, Switzerland; http://www.ilo.org/global/about-the-ilo/press-and-media-centre/press-releases/WCMS_070505/lang--en/index.htm.

25. *The Corporation*. Directed by Mark Achbar and Jennifer Abbott; produced by Mark Achbar and Bart Simpson (Zeitgeist Video, 2004).

26. R. M. Kramer, "The great intimidators," *Harvard Business Review*, February 2006, pp. 1–9.

27. R. Janoff-Bulman, *"Shattered assumptions"* (New York: Free Press, 2002).

28. P. G. Zimbardo, "Stanford prison experiment" http://www.prison exp.org.

29. J. Welch and S. Welch, *Winning* (New York: Harperbusiness, 2005).

30. M. Van Vugt, R. Hogan, and R. B. Kaiser, "Leadership, followership, and evolution: Some lessons from the past," *American Psychologist* 2008, 63(3), 182–196.

31. S. Anderson, C. Collins, S. Pizzigati, and K. Shih, "CEO pay and the great recession: The 17th annual executive compensation survey." Institute for Policy Studies, September 1, 2010.

32. J. Wang, N. Schmitz, E. Smailes, et al. "Workplace characteristics, depression, and health-related presenteeism in a general population sample," *Journal of Occupational and Environmental Medicine* 2010, 52(8), 836–842.

33. P. Chesler, *Woman's inhumanity to woman* (New York: Nation Books, 2002).

34. *Fired!* Written and produced by Annabelle Gurwitch (Shout Factory, LLC, 2006).

35. D. Romano, *The HR toolkit: An indispensable resource for being a credible activist* (New York: McGraw-Hill, 2010).

36. Adam Cohen, CNN-TV interview with Sara Sidner American Morning Show, July 28, 2010. http://amfix.blogs.cnn.com/2010/07/26/workplace-bullying-bill-passes-n-y-senate/.

37. L. Keashly and B. L. Nowell, "Conflict, conflict resolution, and bullying," in *Workplace bullying: Development in theory, research and practice*, 2nd ed., eds. S. Einarsen, H. Hoel, D. Zapf, and C. Cooper (London: Taylor & Francis, 2010).

38. T. Sebok, "Can bullying be mediated?" guest blog for Workplace Bullying Institute, 2010. http://www.workplacebullying.org/2010/12/08/sebok-restorative-justice/.

39. "The Wage Penalty for State and Local Government Employees in New England" by Jeffrey Thompson and John Schmitt. Political Economy Research Institute at the University of Massachusetts Amherst. Working paper series number 232, September, 2010.

About the Authors

Gary Namie (PhD, Social Psychology) has extensive experience as an instructor and professor in college departments of management and psychology, including the University of Southern California, Scripps College, and other colleges. He has won both national American Psychological Association and University of California, Santa Barbara (UCSB), campus teaching awards. At Western Washington University, Namie developed and taught the first university course on bullying at work. He was also a corporate manager for two regional hospital systems and served as the expert witness in the nation's first "bullying" trial in Indiana.

Ruth Namie (PhD, Clinical Psychology) was training director for Sheraton Hotels before her clinical training led to helping chemically dependent individuals and families. Ruth's personal experience was the impetus for the U.S. workplace bullying movement. She has since become an expert on the devastating effects of bullying on targeted workers.

In 1997, the Namies began the research and education organization that became the Workplace Bullying Institute (WBI) based in Bellingham, Washington. They wrote two previous books (*The Bully at Work* and *BullyProof Yourself at Work*). WBI regularly conducts research, including the 2010 and 2007 U.S. surveys of bullying representing all adult Americans. The

Namies' research articles are published in the *Journal of Consulting Psychology, International Journal of Communication, Employee Rights and Employment Policy Journal, Ivey Business Journal,* and *Journal of Employee Assistance.* They also have contributed chapters in the books *Destructive Organizational Communication: Processes, Consequences, and Constructive Ways of Organizing* (Taylor & Francis, 2009) and *Workplace Bullying: Development in Theory, Research and Practice* (2nd edition, Taylor & Francis, 2010).

Ruth and Gary Namie are the best-known individuals associated with workplace bullying in the United States, due in large part, to their public websites devoted to different aspects of education about bullying for individuals, lawmakers, unions, and employers. As the U.S. pioneers, their work has been featured in more than 950 media interviews, including on the *Today Show, Good Morning America, Early Show, Nightline,* CNN, local television news; in the *New York Times, Bloomberg Business Week, USA Today, Washington Post, Los Angeles Times, Wall Street Journal, Toronto Star, Ivey Business Journal, HR Executive, Globe and Mail,* and *American Bar Association;* and on Marketplace Radio, NPR, and CBC radio.

Gary directs the national network of state coordinators, acting as citizen lobbyists, who work to pass into law the anti-bullying Healthy Workplace Bill. Since 2003, 21 states have introduced, but not yet passed, the legislation.

The Work Doctor® is an organizational consulting firm led by the Namies that focuses exclusively on the prevention of workplace bullying. The Namies' Blueprint is a comprehensive system that enables good employers to constrain unacceptable bullying behavior, change corporate culture, and become an industry leader. Canadian and U.S. employers have adopted the system.

The Namies' professional preparation, consulting experience, and unwavering focus on workplace bullying give them an unrivaled, comprehensive perspective of the phenomenon.

Index

Services Provided by the Namies

WBI University training for professionals

An intensive 3-day immersion in workplace bullying with Drs. Gary and Ruth Namie. Designed for professionals in organizational training, human resources, management, union leadership, counseling, psychology, and those considering career change. Participants leave with the license to use WBI materials and the WBI world-leading perspective. **wbiuniversity.com**